DETOX YOUR CAREER

Other titles in the *Career Makers* series

MANAGE YOUR BOSS
8 steps to creating the ideal working relationship
Patrick Forsyth

NEW KID ON THE BLOCK
10 steps to help you survive and thrive in the first
100 days of your new job
Frances Kay

THINK ON YOUR FEET
10 steps to better decision making and problem solving at work
Jeremy Kourdi

Forthcoming titles

THERE'S NO NEED TO SHOUT!
10 steps to communicating your message clearly and effectively
Patrick Forsyth

THE GOOD, THE BAD AND THE DOWNRIGHT DIFFICULT
8 steps to dealing with people you'd rather not
Frances Kay

DETOX YOUR CAREER

10 steps to revitalizing your
job and career

PATRICK FORSYTH

Copyright © 2006 Patrick Forsyth

First published in 2006 by:

Marshall Cavendish Business
An imprint of Marshall Cavendish International (Asia) Private Limited
A member of Times Publishing Limited
Times Center, 1 New Industrial Road
Singapore 536196
T: +65 6213 9300
F: +65 6285 4871
E: te@sg.marshallcavendish.com
Online bookstore: www.marshallcavendish.com/genref

and

Cyan Communications Limited
119 Wardour Street
London W1F 0UW
United Kingdom
T: +44 (0)20 7565 6120
E: sales@cyanbooks.com
www.cyanbooks.com

A CIP record for this book is available from the British Library

ISBN 981 261 815 5 (Asia & ANZ)
ISBN 1-904879-51-9 (rest of world)

Designed and typeset by Cambridge Publishing Management Limited
Printed and bound in Singapore

For Jacqui

May you enjoy your career as much as I have enjoyed,
and continue to enjoy, mine.

THE *CAREER MAKERS* SERIES

NEW REALITIES—ESSENTIAL SKILLS

The world of work has never presented people with a greater challenge.

Business pundits and economists predict a range of varying scenarios for the future of the work environment. But one thing all are sure about—the future will be uncertain. We live in dynamic times. The old world of job security, jobs for life, prescribed ladders of promotion, and gradually increasing success and rewards has gone, replaced by talk of reorganization, downsizing (and calling it rightsizing makes it sound no better), redundancy, teleworking, and portfolio careers. Organizations too must recognize new realities and adopt new approaches to stay ahead in an increasingly competitive world.

For the individual, waiting for things to "get back to normal" simply is not one of the options. No one can guarantee a successful career for themselves, though it is something that everyone can influence to some degree. Indeed it is something that you surely *want* to influence. We all spend a great deal of time at work.
It is important to make sure that time is as enjoyable and rewarding as possible. There is a line in one of John Lennon's songs: *"Life is what happens to you while you're busy making other plans."* It encapsulates a painful thought. Situations in which you must look back and say something to yourself that begins: *"if only . . ."* are perhaps the worst possible positions to get into.

With no rigid, pre-ordained career ladder for the individual to follow, the prospects of success cannot be assumed. Similarly, with turbulent markets for organizations to operate in, and dynamic times ahead, no organization can regard success as a given. The bad news is that there is no magic formula guaranteed to ensure overall success. However, three things are clear:

- Having the right skills and competencies is the foundation to being able to do your job well

- Surviving and thriving in a competitive workplace demands that you work actively at career development

- Only successful individuals create successful organizations

It is these facts that prompt this series of books. The series takes a positive view, examining a range of areas that are not only valuable to achieving results within a particular job, but are also inherent to making good career progress—it reviews not just business skills, but career skills.

So, the individual titles each review their individual topic with an eye on both effectiveness in a job and overall career success. Written by experienced practitioners, they present practical and proven ideas to help you create success in your job, for your organization, and in your career.

Patrick Forsyth

CONTENTS

PREFACE   10

step 1 FIRST PRINCIPLES   14
GETTING TO GRIPS WITH ACTIVE CAREER DEVELOPMENT

step 2 UNDER THE MICROSCOPE   32
GIVING YOURSELF THE BASIS FOR MOVING AHEAD

step 3 PEOPLE   46
GETTING THEM TO HELP (AND NOT HINDER)

step 4 THE POWER OF COMMUNICATIONS   58
MAKING IT WORK FOR YOU

step 5 CAREER SKILLS   84
GIVING YOURSELF AN UNFAIR ADVANTAGE

step 6 ENHANCING YOUR STRENGTHS   100
TRAINING AND DEVELOPMENT AS AN AID TO SUCCESS

step 7 ENSURING EXCELLENCE   118
(AND NOT CONFUSING ACTIVITY WITH ACHIEVEMENT)

step 8 OFFICE POLITICS   140
SURVIVING IN A VOLATILE ENVIRONMENT

step 9 YOUR PROFILE   150
LOOKING SUCCESSFUL

step 10 MOVING ON   162
ONWARD AND UPWARD

AFTERWORD   174

PREFACE

> **"If in the last few years you haven't discarded a major opinion or acquired a new one, check your pulse. You may be dead."**
>
> GELETT BURGESS

The corporate environment in which so many of us work is dynamic. More than ever in the past, change is the order of the day. Certainly, as the series introduction makes clear, the workplace is not the cosy place it was years ago; not that it was ever totally benign. "Corporate jungle" is an increasingly appropriate description and in this hostile territory it is, to paraphrase Charles Darwin, those who are most adaptable to change who survive. Now I am not suggesting you are about to become extinct, and your career may be going well, but a positive and active approach is now demanded of anyone intent on surviving—and achieving ongoing prosperity—in the modern workplace.

So, the first adaptation, and the first principle on which this book is based, is that acceptance of such a conscious and active approach is necessary. The second is that a willingness to consider what that means and work at responses, and initiatives, that better equip you to thrive amid the new realities of the workplace is also necessary. The third is to take suitable action on an *ongoing* basis. Taking a look, or even action, now and then and hoping this will suffice forever should simply not be regarded as an option.

This book is an antidote to personal complacency about your work situation. It is designed to help you review your intentions and goals in the context of the changed, and changing, work environment. It will literally "detox" your career, and allow you to check a whole series of areas in each of which inaction is dangerous. Beyond that, it highlights actions likely to keep you ahead of trouble and ahead of the game in terms of your career progress.

THE INTENDED READER

To be specific: this book is for those who want to enjoy a successful career in business, or indeed in an organization of any sort. Or, more particularly, it is for those who wish to influence their careers toward success. You may be in the early stages of your career, or in midcareer; it is, after all, never too late to take a constructive view of what you are doing and where you are going. Or you may even still be completing your education and getting ready to embark on a career. As career progress tends to be equated with management, the term "manager" is used in the text, though no particular functional area involved is assumed, nor is the precise nature of the employing organization itself. You may be in general management, in sales, marketing, finance, or production or in some specialist area such as computers, personnel, or research.

The emphasis throughout is on those things that have a bearing on what you do, how others will react to what you do, and thus which are likely to have a bearing on your success. Some are best described as "survival techniques." Others go beyond pure survival, and are specific to career development. Still others suggest that you use skills, techniques, or activities necessary to perform your job, utilizing them specifically to serve career development purposes in addition to their normal role. It is not the intention, indeed, could not be in this style of book, to explain every aspect of the general business techniques involved. However, it will help you identify which things you need to become involved with, seek more information about or training in, and which, unless you appreciate their career implications, you might otherwise neglect. Whatever field of business you are in and however high within it you intend to rise, you will find ideas here which will help you build a career more certainly than if the process is left to chance.

TEN KEY QUESTIONS

Specifically, the book is designed to help you answer ten key questions that auditing—detoxing—your career demands:

1. Do you know what you want?

2. Are you aiming high?

3. Is your work environment progress-friendly?

4. Are people you work with and for a career asset?

5. Do you have the skills to progress?

6. Is your profile appropriate for what you want to do?

7. Do you enjoy what you do as much as you wish?

8. Do you get adequately rewarded?

9. Are you ready for action?

10. Do you have an action plan?

Thus the book's intention is to act as a catalyst to your doing well in the job you have and to your continued advancement, whether on up the organization or beyond. To make things straightforward, after all you have a job to do and cannot spend all your time in careerist mode, the review is arranged as a ten-point audit; each chapter reviews a separate range of issues and each can give rise to useful action. Similarly, to allow a check of your current career status, the ten questions are repeated at the end of the book. To be confident of your future you need to be able to address all ten.

Patrick Forsyth
Touchstone Training & Consultancy
28 Saltcote Maltings
Maldon
Essex
CM9 4QP
United Kingdom

"Some people see the future as something that will eventually roll along to them, just like a train pulling into a station. They wait hopefully for this train to bring them what they wish for . . . But the future is not like this. Just as our present is the result of our past, so our future will be the result of our present."

ANNE SPENCER PARRY AND MARJORIE PIZER

step  1

FIRST PRINCIPLES: GETTING TO GRIPS WITH ACTIVE CAREER DEVELOPMENT

"Life is what happens to you while you're busy making other plans."

JOHN LENNON

The quotation on page 15 encapsulates a painful thought. All too often, we are conscious of things happening to us. If they are good things, we are most apt to take them in our stride, either putting them down to our underlying brilliance, or "good luck" but, if they are not good, we tend to blame "bad luck" rather than our own lack of foresight. In the latter case certain things are, with hindsight, clearly predictable and may lead swiftly to our sighing, "If only . . ." (surely a position to avoid ever being in). Similarly, good things that occur may also represent lost opportunities; they are good but could have been better. If we are ready for them or if we are "quick enough on our feet," then we can take more advantage of them.

At the same time, there are some things that we plan, like going away on vacation, and others that we may not see as plannable, almost as we do not try to control tomorrow's weather. Your career is among those important aspects of your life that you will want to influence. It is also something you cannot realistically make go exactly as you want. But that is no reason for not taking every action possible to make it go as near as possible to the way you want it to go. You must not let perfection be the enemy of the good. In other words, just because you will not be Chief Executive tomorrow if you snap your fingers and shout "Promotion!" is no reason for not working at those factors that can take you in the right direction. And, as we shall see, there are many such things.

This book is not about the initial process of obtaining a job (though certain elements involved in so doing occur along the way); it is about planning where you want to go and taking action, both in the way you work in your current job and by other means to ensure you make progress. Such progress may be measured in terms of position, of rewards (financial and otherwise), recognition, responsibility, and authority. Everyone will see rewards in their own way. For some, the trappings of office are more important than to others. For some, money is the only measure. However you measure it, your ability to achieve what you want is not, in the real world, only a question of competency. There are organizations the world over with many people working in them who could do well in a more senior position (there are also some people who are in senior positions and not carrying out their responsibilities very well, and many more who will never rise above a certain level for all their good work). Most people would claim a degree of ambition, but what is it that differentiates between those who do well and move up an organization, who hold management positions, and move on to the senior levels, and others who do less well?

Competency is clearly one factor, but there are others. Some of the additional factors are concerned with skills, some with perceptions—how people are seen—whatever they are, they create a total picture that combines to influence the likelihood of an individual making progress. It is these factors that this book reviews. It does not offer a magic formula. If there was a magic way to ensure that you became rich, famous, irresistible to the opposite sex, and Chief Executive overnight, you would not find it in a book at this price! But you *can* increase the chances of success, and you may be able to increase them significantly.

Of course, it may be that little progress can be made without thought and effort; these are nearly always necessary if anything worth while is to be achieved. But the very fact that many different factors are involved increases the possibilities of your being able to swing the odds more in your favor. Everyone is likely to do better and progress more certainly if they think about it. Of the many things that are referred to in this book some can give *you* an opportunity to make a difference. What is more, the development of a career is essentially a competitive process. Most organizations have a pyramid-shaped structure and, as the old saying has it: *There are more Indians than Chiefs*. You need to appreciate the most common factors: these are things that anyone prepared to spend a little time and effort can achieve, because if you lag in these areas you allow potential advantage to go by default. And you need to find other things that your abilities and outlook allows you to excel in, so that overall you are able to create the right climate for progress.

Career development is NOT AN OPTION, nor is simply being ambitious. In today's competitive commercial environment, active career development is essential. Doing nothing toward sorting out where you are going and how you will get there, not even thinking it through, is a sure recipe for missing opportunities and doing less well than may be possible. This book aims to help you think your career development through in the right way, and to give you some specific ideas and advice as to what works best. Thereafter it is up to you. In every sense, the greatest asset you have in developing your own career is—yourself.

We start with a number of basic principles.

ADOPT THE RIGHT OVERALL APPROACH

In the introduction, the point was made that there is no magic formula that can guarantee that you enjoy a successful career. Here we discuss what may seem a general point, yet it is probably as close to such a magic formula as exists. Career development is an active process. You have to work at it. That is not to say that you have to do nothing else. In fact much of what needs to be done is an integral part of the work you will be doing, only needing a "career-development" focus on it as well as whatever other role it has in your business life to be useful.

Any career is influenced by a thousand and one different factors. The organization you work for, the people you work with and for, and the differing circumstances of each, all affect how you will progress. You cannot possibly predict everything that will occur along the way. What you can do is have a clear idea of the things that will help you as time goes by, so that you can keep a hand on the tiller. Being prepared to work at it is the first step (you no doubt see the need or you would probably not have purchased this book), but you cannot do so in a vacuum. Some analysis of you, your situation, and prospects will be helpful. Also useful, essential is a better word, is a plan; something that can be drawn from the analysis. Both are investigated in a moment. So, the starting point is an appreciation of the necessity for career development, a resolve to work at it systematically that becomes a habit, and then an ongoing study of how you can make a difference and the application of any individual methods that you judge suit your circumstances.

For the most part, the people you hope to emulate have not reached their positions by good fortune. Of course, good luck may have had something to do with it, but it is not something you should rely upon—just sitting back and hoping for a lucky break is *not* career planning—and, if and when such a break does arrive, it needs to be taken advantage of, developed, and made permanent. The only element you can guarantee will always be there to assist you is you. So think of yourself as an active careerist and go on from there.

DECIDE WHAT QUALIFICATIONS YOU NEED

It is said that you cannot have too many qualifications. To an extent this is true, though there are those who become perpetual students and never seem in danger of escaping into the real world at all. Here I want to say something about getting the balance right. First, let us put on one side those qualifications that are mandatory for particular fields of activity; for example, if you wish to be an accountant, you have to pass the necessary exams. There is no decision to make here. If you want to get into a particular field, you must get the required qualifications.

On the other hand, many qualifications are much less specific. How do you know, in advance, what an MBA will do for you, for instance? Such qualifications can be useful. They are not, however, from an employer's point of view, any guarantee of automatic competency. In my own field of marketing, there are certainly people with paper qualifications in the subject who have no marketing flair at all. Qualifications do give some signs though. For instance, they:

● Impart a great deal of knowledge

- Improve thinking (developing approaches to, say, problem solving)

- Develop skills, though usually much less than gathering knowledge (certain courses blend different elements very well, as with many programs nowadays that combine a management degree with language study)

- Give you a "label"

Even the last one needs some thought. Different qualifications are seen in a different light. This applies to both the qualification and the institution from which it comes. There is a compromise to be made here for those at the stage of seeking qualifications—where will you be accepted? Where geographically do you want to be? How long is the course? What are the financial considerations? And so on. This kind of consideration is even more difficult if you are contemplating a post-graduate qualification, perhaps one that needs a break from work or private funding. When employers talk about what they want from their employees, they tend to link closely together "qualifications and experience"—this is what goes on a C.V. also—and they do go together; in other words, while you are studying you do not get any work experience and vice versa. Part time courses exist to mix the two factors, but you may find the perception of them is also different (less?) than of full time equivalents. So another balance that must be struck is between what advantages you will gain from, say, a year working, and the same year spent on something more academic.

One more point: there is also a fashion element in how some of these things are regarded, with one institution seeming to be in favor at one moment, then another. All in all, you need to think long and hard about what will suit you best, what will give you the greatest career advantage in terms of both what you will learn and how the qualification will be seen, and then make a decision remembering both the saying that "you cannot have too many qualifications" and the various practicalities.

INSIST ON A JOB DESCRIPTION

The need for a job description may be obvious, especially given the power of employment legislation, but curiously I still often come across people and organizations where the whole area of job definition (and appraisal, which is touched on later) is ill defined or non-existent. First, it is important from the point of view of any organization. If managers are to manage, and manage effectively, then the organization structure, and who does what, must be thought through, agreed, and documented, and the whole process must link with the corporate objectives both centrally and at the level of individual divisions or departments. What is more, whatever the formal benefits of a system of job definition, evaluation, and appraisal (and they are undoubtedly a vital tool for personnel and other considerations), they are—or should be—working documents. In other words, they should act as a guide to individual managers and staff in day-to-day operational terms. You will gather that I am in favor of job descriptions.

But consider it too from the individual's point of view. Surely everybody wants to know whether they are doing a good job or not—a sense of achievement is, after all, a basic human motivation about any work. How can you possibly gauge if you are being successful if the job in question is ill defined? It is not possible, and thus leaves a sense of dissatisfaction. More important still from the point of view of career development, progress in a career is perhaps, more than any other single factor, dependent on job performance, and other people need a clear view of what this is in your case. As the old maxim has it, *never confuse activity with achievement*; progress is so often dependent on *evidence* of achievement and that in turn is dependent on knowing what is expected of you and comparing how things go with this. A job description should not be restrictive; indeed, it should be dynamic and if it needs changing and updating regularly, so be it. It is, after all, a working document.

So, in any job you do, make sure you have a clear, written, job description. I would go further: you should have one, everyone who reports to you should have one, and whoever you report to should have one. In fact, the whole process works best if your staff sees yours, and everyone else's, and you see that for your boss. That way everyone knows not only what everyone else is doing, but also how the various responsibilities interrelate.

OBTAIN THE RIGHT REWARDS

Job satisfaction is desirable, important, and makes the inevitably less attractive parts of any job worth while; but it will not pay the rent. Whatever you do, you no doubt expect a fair reward for it. Fair, in this context, normally means a comparison with your peers in the same organization and with those in comparable positions in other organizations such as your direct competitors in the commercial world.

A moment's thought shows that money is important in a number of different ways. It is a means of purchasing basic needs (and less basic needs too for that matter!). It is a symbol of the worth the organization places on someone, it is a means of comparison, as stated above, and a reward in itself. But it is not the only reward. Most executive jobs involve increasingly complicated remuneration "packages" where in addition to the salary you may receive:

- A company car

- Incentive or bonus payments

- Pension scheme (one to look at very carefully these days)

- Share options

- Special terms loans

- Allowances (that do more than cover the costs incurred in conducting business on behalf of your employer)

- Discounts on company products or services (which will be more valuable in, say, an airline than in a firm manufacturing sewage treatment equipment or some such)

- Health and other insurance

- Group incentives

Some of these may well be linked to performance, and there may be further elements that you can think of that are favored in your work field. Fashions vary with regard to such benefits and current practice tends to vary in different countries and change over time (as with company cars, much in evidence in Britain but nowadays being made much less valuable because of the way they are treated for tax).

Two further points need to be made here. First, do consider any and all the other rewards that should perhaps be weighed in the balance. For example, one job may pay less in the short term and yet offer unique training advantages that make it the best choice for the long term.

Secondly, do not be afraid to negotiate these kinds of benefit. Certainly once you reach a certain level, most organizations expect the package to have some element of tailoring. If you do not raise certain issues, they may not get an airing at all. Similarly, you may want to expand the agenda and include things that the company has never even thought about previously. One example of this, which rather appealed to me, concerned an acquaintance of mine seconded to Singapore from London for three years. He was offered but felt no need for a car in such a small place full of cheap taxis, but to keep himself independently mobile he negotiated a company motorbike! The saving in cost he took as money, and this suited him well. Such might not suit everyone, but it is a good example of someone being kept happy by a policy that accommodates the individual. A final, warning point: negotiation is fine but you may come to a point where it is better and more valuable to your future career not to push further but to maintain good relations with those with whom you are negotiating. Principles do not pay the rent, and in some economies it is a real risk to push things so far that your job becomes in doubt. [There is a short section on negotiation in another title I have written for this series, *Manage Your Boss*.]

TAKE A CHANCE

Here, I am not advocating an approach that throws caution to the wind, and you must consider your temperament and approach to risk, but chances do sometimes have to be taken. There is an old saying: *Don't be afraid to go out on a limb if that is where the fruit is.* Trees are high and climbing may be dangerous, but it makes a fair point. You need to consider this in several ways:

- **Perception:** How do you want to be seen within your organization? At one end of the scale, there is out and out recklessness, which may be linked in the mind with such characteristics as unthinking or ill considered. Such an image may be wrong for you. So too may be that of a staid, predictable, and perhaps, as a result, less innovative person. You must consider where on the scale you should be; and even so you can make the occasional exception

- **Job skills:** Taking a chance is something that you have to think about in terms of your job and the action and decisions it demands you take. Some decisions are a risk, and not everything goes right for companies and the people who work in them. Research, consideration, and careful decision making must usually precede any significant action but there is still a place for a chance to be taken. A reputation for a reliable business instinct is good for anyone's image, but when this is there it is usually balanced by sound homework

- **Career decision:** I know of people who have taken awful career decisions and gone through a bad patch as a result, and a few who have become stuck in something that they dislike or at least to which they are indifferent. Equally you may be put off a course of action because of the risk, or what you see as a step into unknown territory, and the fear of that clouds the arguments in favor. In my own case, setting up my own business was the best thing I ever did in my career (my mistake, before anyone thinks I am claiming perfection, was not doing it earlier)—but it was also certainly the riskiest

So you must balance security and good sense, care and consideration in decision making with those other occasions when you have finally, as it were, to close your eyes and step out into the unknown. If you then open them and find you are where you want to be, it is very satisfying. Though it will not always be the right thing to do, or work out if you do it, taking a chance is likely to be something you have to do on occasion. Take the right ones and they can surely jump your career ahead.

GET IT IN WRITING

Far be it for me to suggest that employers are not to be trusted, but, realistically, some are not trustworthy. This may be a small number and it may be for reasons of error or ineptness more than it is vindictive, but it is worth taking note of—and indeed the road to the law courts is populated by people who have not done so. Circumstances change; a simple agreement made with the Managing Director and owner may be worth little five years later when the company has been sold to a multinational conglomerate without a single scruple in any of its many parts.

The moral is that you should have written (and contractual) agreement to your appointment and the terms and conditions that accompany it. Assured by the publishers that this book will be on sale throughout the world, I do not propose to go into the detail of employment legislation, which varies a good deal in different locations. Suffice to say you should check what makes sense in the environment in which you work (checking twice as carefully if you plan to work overseas), and insist on something appropriate in writing.

The following items may contribute to the contract:

- The details in a letter of appointment

- A statement of terms and conditions

- Contents of collective agreements, rules, etc. (in some cases agreed with a trade union or employee body of some sort)

- The custom and practice of the organization

- Statutory protections (those applying locally)

The list that follows shows typical topics for agreement and written confirmation.

- Who the parties to the contract are (name of the organization and the employee)

- The rate, method, and timing of remuneration

- Hours of work

- Terms and conditions of work

- Vacation entitlement (including national vacation treatment)

- Pension arrangements

- Length of notice (which may vary depending on who discontinues the employment)

- The employee's job title

- Disciplinary rules (and arrangements that go with them, such as arbitration)

- Grievance resolution procedures

This can only be an example and I again urge that you check what will be right for your contract of employment and allow for any special situations. For example, if you are or become a director you may wish to have a written list of your legal and financial obligations. You may also feel more comfortable to have a note of any "standing instruction" relating to a range of things from expenses to how a company car may be used. Most of the time such documents are not operationally necessary; however, if problems or disagreements occur, they can be invaluable.

SEEK SOUND FINANCIAL ADVICE

Whatever other reasons there are for working, from satisfaction to philanthropy, clearly for most people money comes high on the list. Now you may not want to maximize earnings in isolation from other benefits. Some jobs offer high rewards but unacceptable terms, conditions, or risk, so what you opt to do is often a compromise in this respect. But you are likely not only to want to see a fair return for what you do but also to make the most of what return you do receive. Thus, unless you are so qualified yourself, you may need a financial adviser.

Now I hope it is not too much of an insult to say that financial advisers are a mixed bunch: some are close relatives of sharks; others are an invaluable asset to any career. They are principally useful in terms of:

- **Tax:** Most tax systems mean even small complications in your life need careful sorting and, often in such circumstances, if the sorting is not done, you end up paying more tax than is necessary

- **Investment:** If you do so well in your career that you begin to save significant amounts, then advice as to where you can lodge such money for the best return and the level of safety that your life demands may well be useful

- **Complexities:** There is a range of other things that may occur—you could be involved in a profit sharing scheme, a management buyout, or a share option scheme. Again, if you are like me, you may value some advice

Having said that, you must decide what kind of adviser suits you and then choose carefully. You may consider value in continuity, with one person acting in this role over some years, or want to ring the changes or use several people for different areas of advice. For some, an accountant serves all these roles. Sometimes such people prove helpful in ways that were difficult to anticipate until they occurred.

DO NOT BE LED BY EVENTS

One of those business terms that now pervade the English language is the word "proactive"; everything seems to need a proactive approach or a proactive process. Whatever happened to "active"? Perhaps the emphasis here should be on the reverse—do not become unthinkingly responsive.

Consider: you have set clear objectives, you have a plan and have thought it all through, and then something happens. It may be anything—someone leaves the company unexpectedly, there is a merger or takeover, a new development, overseas expansion, or even a death. It is certainly something you could either not have allowed in your planning, or something that would have been very difficult to predict in terms of when it might occur. This kind of thing will often need to prompt rapid thinking, but may less often necessitate rapid action. Of course, there may be times when unless an opportunity is grasped very fast it will be gone. In this case, there still needs to be some thinking even if it must be less in depth and even more rapid. You do need to consider all the issues or you may find yourself repenting at leisure. The first task is perhaps to consider whether the urgency is real or apparent.

We all have 20/20 hindsight. It is always easy to look back and judge if something was right or wrong. However, it may be rather different at the time when facts may be limited and the outcome much less clear. I am not sure I can offer a definitive route through this kind of circumstance, except to say most decisions are better and more sure if given a little real thought, and that the temptation to take a risk in case an opportunity is missed forever is great. Certainly doing your homework—the analysis and planning I have advocated—makes it more likely that you will be able to make good decisions rapidly when the need arises, in which case it is another reason why such planning is worth while. Otherwise what seems like a good idea at the time can lead you badly off track and away from your plan and intentions; and that may work out or it may not. An active approach that includes real planning is more likely to cope with the real world and allow you to deal with any random factors in a way that is most certain to further your career aims.

BE OPTIMISTIC

I have a theory (backed only by observation!) that optimists tend to do better than pessimists or those who inherently worry about everything. Thinking of this reminds me of a tale from medieval times that makes a good point: a courtier is condemned to life imprisonment for a small misdemeanor. Languishing in his cell, a thought struck him and he sent a message to the King promising that if he was released, he would work day and night and, within a year, he would teach the King's favorite horse to talk.

This amused the King, and he ordered the courtier be released and sent to work in the royal stables. The courtier's friends were pleased to see him released, but frightened for him too; after all, horses do not talk, however much training they get. "What will you do?" they asked. "So much can happen in a year," he replied, "I may die, the King may die; or, who knows—the horse may talk!" Who knows indeed; it is a nice story and I for one tend to believe that by the time the year was up he had thought of some other ruse. Certainly it seems to me that this describes the level of optimism to have. Of course, you must never rely only on "waiting for something to turn up," but if you plan your life and career practically, taking the kinds of views, approaches, and actions advocated in this book *and* do so in an optimistic way, that is not only better—you are likely to be more comfortable with it also.

DEALING WITH SUCCESS

Yes, having talked about optimism in the last section, I think it is right to deal with success early on in the book. The point I want to make is a simple one: do not broadcast your success in an arrogant or unpleasant way. However much you may admire successful people (and want to emulate them), those who crow about their success are almost universally resented. Modesty is a virtue, as Oliver Hereford said: *Modesty: the gentle art of enhancing your charm by pretending not to be aware of it*, and there is sense in this, for understatement can be more powerful, especially when an overpowering approach can have the reverse effect of what is intended.

This is true of major factors, like significant promotion, and of smaller successes; no one likes someone who is always crowing just to score points. This leads us to another related point: promotion can mean you are working with people as your subordinates with whom you used to work as colleagues. This can be awkward for both parties, or at least it can feel awkward, and you have to work out a way of dealing with this situation. The right balance is important. You probably can no longer be "one of the gang," as it were, but may find it useful to remain sufficiently close to take advantage of the best of the old relationships (importantly without playing favorites), while creating a new basis for the majority of your dealings with the people concerned. If your success is significant, people will know without your overdoing the hype; some self-publicity is helpful to a career, but it must never be such that it is perceived as arrogant and, by implication, putting others down.

Everything, as has already been said, contributes more to your career progression if it stems from and reflects some sound analysis and planning.

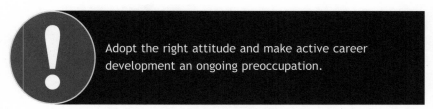

Adopt the right attitude and make active career development an ongoing preoccupation.

Having given a flavor of what is involved in active career development, it is to this we turn in the next chapter.

step **2**

UNDER THE MICROSCOPE: GIVING YOURSELF THE BASIS FOR MOVING AHEAD

"If you're not planning where you want to be, what reason or excuse do you have for worrying about being nowhere.**"**

TOM HOPKINS

The earliest "career plan" I can remember having in mind for myself when I was still at school was to be an astronomer. This was born of a passionate interest in the subject rather than any link with my actual or likely abilities. This was way back, when sex was safe and the Russians were dangerous, and when the careers master at my school was only really well able to discuss Latin verbs. Even so, once I began to check out what might be necessary, realism soon set in and, though my interest continues, my career took other paths. Career planning, perhaps sadly, does not mean conjuring up plans that are no more than pie in the sky, but proceeding on a clear, accurate, and honest assessment of what might be possible.

This means looking inward.

KNOW YOURSELF

Though we all like to think we know ourselves, this may not be entirely true. It is easy to make assumptions, to leave key elements out of the picture and so, as a result, misjudge how our current profile lends itself to career progress, and just what sort of progress may be possible. Assumptions can link back to past experience, fears, bad experiences, or a host of things. An example of just how much we may misjudge ourselves perhaps makes the point.

As a trainer, one of the things I do regularly is conduct courses designed to improve people's ability to make formal presentations. One category of person who attends (usually told to attend by their employer) has never done this, or done very little of it, hates the thought of it because they know they cannot do it well and would much prefer to avoid the whole subject and the task. Yet these same people, or certainly many of them, prove to be quick and effective at learning how to do a good job on a presentation. They find there is a difference between not knowing how to go about something and inherently not being able to do it. With the knowledge of how to tackle it, and with practice, this can be added to their list of skills. Yet previously they may have been avoiding tasks, jobs, even promotional opportunities, that were likely to put them in a position where they would have to do this seemingly worrying task.

There may well be aspects of your nature and ability that you think about in this way, so the first step to deciding a route forward is to look at where you are at the moment. This should be done systematically and honestly and you may find it useful to keep some notes of what the thinking produces. The next several sections lead you through a suitable progression of self-analysis that assesses your skills, work values, personal characteristics, and also your non-work characteristics.

ASSESS YOUR SKILLS

You might be surprised at how many skills you have. Remember that it is quite possible that things you do and take for granted you can in fact only do because of considerable, and perhaps unusual, experience. So list all the things for which you have an aptitude. Some general headings under which to group your abilities may be:

- **Communications:** everything from writing a report to issuing instructions

- **Influencing:** that includes persuading, negotiating, and promoting ideas

- **Managing:** everything to do with managing other people

- **Problem solving:** analyzing and drawing conclusions and coming up with solutions

- **Creativity:** generating ideas, seeing things in the round, having an open mind

- **Social skills:** not just relating to people but having insight, helping others, facilitating

- **Numerical:** handling figures, statistics, accounts, etc. and other numerical data

- **Special skills:** here such skills as speaking a foreign language, unusual technical skills, and so on should be mentioned

- **Computer literacy:** this is so much part of so many jobs these days, albeit to different levels, that it deserves its own heading

At any stage of your career, you should have the full picture in mind and also documented. Decide which headings along the lines of the above are right for you, and make some notes. It might be an interesting exercise to do this now, and again when you have read the whole book. Some of the topics listed above will recur as headings in their own right and you may view things differently after a review of how important some of the skill areas are from a career point of view.

ASSESS YOUR WORK VALUES

It is not enough to know what skills you have. These must be viewed alongside your work values. Do you, for instance, have:

- A strong need to achieve

- A need for a high salary

- High work interest requirements

- A liking for doing something "worth while"

- A desire to do something creative

- Specific requirements (such as to travel, to be independent, innovative, or part of a team)?

A wide range of permutations may be involved here and they may change over time. For example, travel may be attractive to the young and single but less so to people who have young children, then it may become more attractive again when a family is older. Make notes here too.

ASSESS YOUR PERSONAL CHARACTERISTICS

Most people do not change their habits and ways, at least not dramatically and certainly not without effort, once they are old enough to be into a career. You need to assess yourself in this respect and do so honestly. Are you innovative, positive, optimistic, hard working, prepared to take risks? What sort of a person, in fact, are you? There may be a clash here: in thinking through your work values you feel that you may be suited to, and want to be involved in, something with considerable cut and thrust, innovating, creative, and generally with you working at the leading edge. But, an honest assessment of yourself may show that, whatever the superficial or status attraction of this option, it is just not really you. Risk taking is not your thing and a different, perhaps more supportive, role is where you are likely to excel most. Again list what you feel is relevant about yourself here.

ASSESS YOUR NON-WORK CHARACTERISTICS

One way or another, work and social life have to coexist. They may do so peaceably, or there may be conflicts between them. It is not automatically necessary to career success to be a workaholic, though a strictly 9 to 5 attitude to the job is perhaps not recommended either. And on the positive side, work and interests or hobbies may overlap constructively, the one teaching you something about the other. There are questions to be asked here too:

- What are your family circumstances?

- Where do you need to live?

- How much time can you spend away from home?

- What are your other responsibilities and interests?

Consider family and interests specifically:

- **Family:** If you have a partner, wife, or husband then priorities may need to be set, because career-building priorities can clash. It is, sadly, perfectly possible to arrive successfully at the top of the heap—a success in business—but with home, family, and happiness in ruins. This may sound dramatic, but the issues here are worth some serious thought. Not least, there are times when career decisions must be made fast or opportunities will be lost. If the relationship between home, family, and work has never been discussed, then the man who comes home from the office to tell his wife: *I have this great new opportunity with the company, but it means living in Hong Kong for two years* is in for some heated debate, especially if he has promised to go back to the office the next day with a decision. Such situations occur at every stage of a career, are not dependent on which half of a partnership instigates them, and are made more complicated when both partners work

- **Interests:** Interests are an important issue. All work and no play is, for most, a bad thing. You need to look at your interests and hobbies alongside the job and your future career intentions. Can they move forward together? How much time do you want to put into both hobbies and work? These are not easy questions and must be worked out over a period of time. Even so there may come times when there are clashes. If you have thought it all through, and discussed it with other family members as appropriate, then transient problems are more likely to be just that—transient

There are no right or wrong answers here and I would not presume to give advice. The amount of time and energy a job needs to take up and what must be left for other things varies between individuals and rightly so; otherwise, it would be a dull old world if we were all the same. The smooth planning of these issues certainly helps you make career decisions more easily and more promptly than would otherwise be the case. And for most people, success in life means career and private life working reasonably compatibly together, whatever the demands of the job at any particular moment. It may be worth listing characteristics alongside their compatibility with your job here as part of the overall analysis.

All this information forms the basis for much of the subsequent thinking that is necessary as you consider how you may take action through the way you work and what you think and do so as to build your career successfully. Opportunities and your real circumstances constantly have to be compared. Some career paths will play to your strengths, others will not, and some will cause a clash of objectives that will be problematic or will simply not be open to you because of your mix of talents and abilities (though this last is something you can work at correcting).

The picture you build up here, and your notes, are solely for *your own* benefit. Some of the facts and information may also be useful at appraisals and in the documentation and discussion that may be necessary if you wish to change employer. These are issues returned to later.

OBTAIN PROFESSIONAL CAREER GUIDANCE

Sometimes, the problem appears that as you try to analyze both yourself and the path you want to take, you can come to no real conclusion as to what will suit you best in the future. In this case, it may be worth seeking professional assistance. An example from my own circumstances may make a point clearer.

I came from a background that had no links with the commercial or business world. My father was in the medical profession and, once he had got over the shock of my wanting to go into "industry," insisted that I should first go to an organization (in London) called the Vocational Guidance Association. This body undertakes to test the aptitudes of a person and match them to the type of job and career that seem most suited to the individual concerned. As my father was paying, I agreed to go, and found myself subjected to a battery of psychometric tests that lasted, as I recall, most of a day. I returned home and a report cataloguing what little ability I had at that stage arrived a few days later.

To cut a long story short, I did go into industry (initially into publishing) and cannot now remember what difference, if any, the report made. What I do remember is finding it many years later when I moved house. It described the nature of the job they had felt I would most enjoy, and I found it matched *exactly* those things with which I was involved at that time. I have always had a greater respect for such services since. An objective view is sometimes useful, and while there is no test that will magically put you into a career where success will follow inevitably because the match between you and what you are doing is so good that there is no other possible result, the prompt to your thinking such analysis can provide may be very useful.

A range of such services are available in most large cities and they are by no means only designed for those moving from education to a first job (the time I did my tests) but can be useful at any stage of a career where you wish to check how your plan is progressing and whether you are going in a direction that is likely to produce job satisfaction. Choose a good adviser (by no means everyone who offers career advice and testing is good) and this may, for some people, be a useful check at a particular stage of their career.

MATCH YOUR ANALYSIS OF YOURSELF WITH MARKET DEMANDS

Whatever picture your various self-analysis exercises build up, it must match realistically with the demands made by employers in the marketplace. Let me put that more specifically: it must match up with the demands made by employers in the section of industry and commerce in which you intend to excel. So, while there are perhaps generally desirable characteristics that we might list such

as being adaptable to change (or able to prompt it), flexible, or thorough, or productive, and so on, there will be more specific characteristics in terms of abilities and nature that will be demanded in a particular field. Indeed, a certain characteristic may be an asset in one area and frowned on in another, as something like creativity might be differently regarded in an advertising agency and a more traditional business. Similarly, what for some is drive and initiative, others will regard as aggressive and self-seeking.

Two points arise from this. First, having analyzed yourself and your intended field (even if you are already in it), you must aim to cultivate the profile for success in that field; or, for some, to react to such analysis showing that you are not well suited in a way that encourages the possibility of success in a particular area. The better the match, the better the chances that your profile will allow you to do well, and progress along your chosen path.

But a good match is not, by itself, sufficient. As I said there is a second point here. An anecdote will perhaps illustrate this second point best. A good friend of mine has a son who had just left acting school and was intent on carving out a career on the stage. I went to see a play he was in at a small London "fringe" theater; a production in which the cast were all young people starting out on their careers. His performance seemed to me excellent, and I said as much to my friend later. "What else did you notice?" he asked and, when I could not think what he meant, he commented, "The whole of the cast was excellent." His point was that talent was not going to be the only factor in his son's possible success. He is good, but he has to get ahead of a strong field to rise to the rank of star.

So it is in many fields. Just having the right qualifications and aptitudes is rarely sufficient—others have them too—you have to have them in the right amount and at the right level; and they must show. Then, with some luck and if you work at it, you may carve out success for yourself. But never make the mistake of thinking this happens in a vacuum—it happens with others around you trying to do similar things. Knowing how well you match up is, nevertheless, a good starting point—one worth some thought.

SUM UP YOUR ANALYSIS AND FORM CLEAR OBJECTIVES

Every management guru has their own version of the premise that every business must have a plan or, as it is sometimes put: *If you do not know where you are going, any road will do.* It is true; it does make a difference. As it is with any business—so it is with any career. This really is common sense, and yet conversely it is so very easy to wake up one day and find that what we have been thinking of as planning is actually only bowing to the inevitable and, if it looks good, taking the credit for it.

Having said that objectives are important, another point should be made: they must be flexible. Life in all its aspects, certainly in business, is dynamic. Objectives cannot be allowed to act as a straitjacket, yet we need their guidance, so their potential for acting to fix things should not be regarded as a reason not to have them.

In business, people talk of "rolling" plans. By this is meant a plan that is reasonably clear and comprehensive for the shorter term, then sets out broad guidelines and further ahead has only main elements clearly stated. As time goes by, the plan can be updated and advanced into the future. With your career in mind, you will find a similar approach works well. In the short term, when you can anticipate more of what may happen, the detail of how you intend to proceed is clearer; further ahead you have notes on the outline strategy and key issues.

Remembering to say: *My objective is to become a Marketing Director* is not much help without some clear actions and steps along the way. Objectives should be SMART. This well-known mnemonic stands for specific, measurable, achievable, realistic, and timed, thus:

- **Specific**—expressed clearly and precisely

- **Measurable**—it must be possible to tell if you have achieved it (the difference between saying you want to be "very successful" or "Marketing Director")

- **Achievable**—it must not be so difficult as to be pie in the sky, otherwise the plan that goes with it similarly becomes invalid and of no practical help in taking things forward

- **Realistic**—it must fit with your self-analysis and be what you want; it might be a valid objective to aim for something possible but not ideal (promotion might be possible within a department, but your real intention is to get out beyond that)—this will not be helpful. Action is needed with more ambitious objectives in mind

- **Timed**—this is important, objectives are not to be achieved "eventually" but by a particular moment: when do you aim to be Marketing Director, this year, next year, or when?

There is no need for elaborate documentation here. Any objectives and any plans are purely for your own guidance, but a few notes on paper may be useful and there are times (such as appraisal or when training is contemplated) when it may be useful to think of current events alongside the notes you have made.

Any such documentation may be seen as a chore and therefore perhaps rejected. There is surely always something more important to do. The first time you do it, making some notes will take a few minutes. So be it. But thereafter you are merely adding to, or subtracting from, or slightly adapting what is recorded, and keeping the overall picture up to date. A single note that might otherwise be forgotten can lead to an action that makes a real difference. It may seem obvious at the time, but months later only a note may remind us of something significant. The process takes very little time on an ongoing basis and is well worth while.

If you not only know which road you should be on, but have also taken steps to make sure you go purposeful along it, that is a good start. It certainly helps answer the first two of the ten questions posed early on: "Do you know what you want?" and "Are you aiming high?"

Base all your career development activity on sound analysis, clear thinking, and specific objectives.

step 3

PEOPLE:
GETTING THEM TO HELP
(AND NOT HINDER)

"People who need people are the luckiest people in the world."

BOB MERRILL

If you take the people out of business, then there is little left. People issues in career development show themselves in many ways and there is an overlap here between this and communication and management, both dealt with in their own sections. Career development is an interactive process, and not something you can do in isolation. Here we review a number of people factors that, whether simple or more complex, must not be forgotten and can assist practically with making your career development activity successful.

CREATE AND KEEP A PEOPLE FILE

Problems, opportunities, and people go together. So often when something occurs and you need information, assistance, or advice, the first thought that comes to mind is related to a person: "They'll know," you say to yourself, and then you think again. You can see them in your mind's eye. You know you met them at that conference you attended in Penang, or was it Hong Kong? You had a meal together, you . . . but what was their name? What company did they work for? Where is their business card? You cannot find the name and something that might be sorted in two minutes on the telephone ends up taking an hour. We all do it.

In some ways, no great harm is done. After all, you cannot keep in touch with everyone and it is difficult to know who will be useful in five years' time (remember, career development is a long-term process). But it is probably better to note too many names than to miss good ones. Therefore, you need a people file. This is little more than an address book or a file for business cards, though these days it may well be electronic. It needs to record some information about each person; just enough so that you can call something to mind about them. For instance, you might record:

- The date you met

- Where you met

- The circumstances of meeting (did you sit next to them on a flight or meet them at a conference?)

- Whether you were introduced by a third party (and if so, who that person was)

- Contact details: name, position, company, address, etc.

Plus something about them (*knows all about regression analysis or can recommend a good restaurant in Tokyo*) as appropriate.

There can be no half-measures here. It must be done systematically, it must be done regularly (it is amazing how quickly some of the detail about someone is forgotten), and it must include everyone that may be useful to you in the future. You can always prune it a little over the months and years so that it remains manageable. There is an old saying that *it is not what you know, but who you know* that matters in life. If there is any truth in this (and there must be) you have to know who you know. Such a system is not an option in career development; it is a prerequisite.

USE NETWORKING

Before we networked, we kept in touch. It is no good having a good network of contacts safely noted (see above) and then not keeping them "live." You have to keep in touch. It matters less how this is done than that it should happen. The frequency will vary among your list of contacts: some only need a card once a year, at Christmas or New Year perhaps; others need to be called a couple of times every month. And some will contribute to the frequency of contact by contacting you; networking is a two-way street.

Sometimes the contact is social; sometimes it is based on a specific request for help and information; sometimes it is unashamed brain-picking.

Before he retired, I used to see an American consultant regularly. He would call up and say he was in town and suggest a lunch or, more often, breakfast. He was a nice guy and it was always good to see him. It was also enormously stimulating. He could pack more ideas, more creative thinking, and more examples to back up the points he made into what was essentially a social contact than anyone I have ever met. An hour and a half with him was like a mini-seminar and it was tiring; you did not realize how much you were thinking and concentrating until you came away from the session. I learned a great deal from him over the years, but he did too; he was an unashamed brain-picker of the highest order. Good networking is like this. It is interesting, it is fun, and yet we learn from it and thus keeping up with people can be a constructive process.

The only downside is that it is time consuming and you have to balance the need to keep your contacts live with the other time pressures in your job and life. One thing is sure, the old principle of two heads being better than one can work well, so this activity can pay dividends—speaking for myself I have received three unsolicited job offers from such contacts over my career, and I accepted two of them!

MIX IN THE RIGHT CIRCLES

The last two sections have commented on who you know, keeping a note of them, and keeping in touch. Now we turn to how you get to know them in the first place, or at least some of them. You need to work at cultivating contacts. Just where and how this is done will depend on the nature of your job and the kind of business you are in, but some general principles apply.

Internally you need to take an interest in the organization at large—who does what, who runs what and knows what. Most organizations have an informal communications network as important as the formal structure (see "Use the grapevine" in Step 4) and this just means that in a large organization there is quite a bit of ground to cover. On the basis that you only get out of something what you put in, it is worth seeking opportunities to contribute in ways that mix you with the right people. What committees, working parties, and project teams should you be on? Some will be very useful, putting you in touch with the prime movers and giving you an opportunity to demonstrate your competency. Others are a waste of time and what is more if you get a reputation for being perpetually on such groups it will not do your credibility any good at all. Some will be contentious and you may have to consider the wisdom of being part of the team that, say, moved the office from its prestigious quarters into what many regard as a slum on some distant industrial park, even if it did save a great deal of money. You can no doubt think of other examples. Such well-chosen activity is sensible and useful.

Externally the same kind of thinking applies. For example, what should you belong to and participate in—the local management institute; trade, professional, and technical bodies; and other interest groups; clubs? There may be sense in something from all or some of these categories. Again pick carefully, get involved where this is more useful than simply belonging and turning up at meetings, and work out an order of priorities as you are unlikely to be able to do everything.

The moral here is that just sitting in your office, even if you are doing an excellent job, does not give you such a high profile as operating and being seen to operate across a wider canvas. When opportunities come up, perhaps in discussion, among a group of senior managers you want your credentials to come readily to mind. It helps therefore to be in those minds, preferably filed in a number of different places. The first necessity, before any such opportunity is likely to be aimed your way, is quite simple—to be remembered.

RECRUIT A MENTOR

One of the motivations for a manager, or at least for some managers, is the satisfaction of helping people develop and of seeing them do well. I was, looking back, very lucky in that two of the people I worked for very early in my career were like this. I learned a great deal from both and learned it very much quicker than would otherwise have been the case. I am not, on the other hand, at all sure that if I had not had this luck I would have had the wits to seek out such assistance. I suspect that my career planning may have been too naive in those days.

The ideal mentor is sufficiently senior to have knowledge, experience, and influence. They need the process to appeal to them, and they need to have time to put into the process; this need not be great, the key thing is to have the willingness to spend some time regularly helping someone else. If your line manager and your mentor are one and the same person, that might be ideal, but it is not essential. Usually, if such a relationship lasts, it will start out one way—they help you—and become more two-way over the years; perhaps the person on the mentor side makes the decision to help rather on the basis of this anticipated possibility.

After the first few years of a career, there is no reason why you cannot have regular contact with a number of people where in each case the relationship is of this nature. This can take various forms. In my own case, for instance, my work in marketing overlaps sometimes with the area of market research. While I know a good deal about aspects of this, certainly in terms of what can be done with it, I have no real strength in the techniques involved. But I have a research mentor: someone who can help and advise me in this particular field. This is very useful and works on the basis of a swap, in other words he helps in that way and I am able (I hope) to advise and assist him in other ways. This is a not uncommon basis.

This kind of thing should be regarded as really very different from, and very much more than, networking. The nature and depth of the interaction and the time and regularity of it is much more extensive. This is not primarily a career assistance process in the sense of someone who will give you a leg up the organization through recommendation or lobbying, though this can of course occur. It is more important in helping develop the range and depth of your competencies and this in turn acts to boost your career.

As a final example, I know very well I would not do the writing I now do (including this book!) if it were not for the regular help and cajoling of one of my mentors. It makes a difference, and a very positive one at that.

Note: it should be said also that the relationship you have with your manager—your boss—is vital too. Some aspects of this are touched on here, for example in discussing performance appraisals on page 78. Beyond that see my book *Manage Your Boss*, another title in the *Career Makers* series.

LET YOUR SECRETARY HELP

Do you have a secretary? If the answer is no, then the sooner you can organize to have one the better. If you do, or when you get one, make absolutely sure that you get an efficient one; and then work at the relationship, because without any doubt a good secretary is a decided and positive career asset.

Being a "good secretary" sounds straightforward enough; however, the ideal characteristics are daunting to say the least. The role demands administrative efficiency, sound writing skills (backed up by typing, perhaps shorthand, and computer and/or word processing skills), and the ability to cope with a growing range of office equipment from fax to modem. In addition, she (it is more often she) must be hard-working, numerate, tactful, persistent, charming, and committed—that report will not be ready in 24 hours just because she is paid to do it. And it helps if she is clairvoyant, has a memory like a computer, two pairs of hands, the patience of a saint, and is fluent in several languages including whichever one is lurking somewhere within her employer's illegible handwriting!

Given support, which includes everything from not blaming things on her—*My secretary forgot to remind me*—to taking time to communicate and tell her what is going on, why, and how things need to work out and therefore be handled, a good and involved secretary can be a great career asset. One point before investigating this further: secretaries seem to be a widely under-utilized resource. Among other things I sometimes conduct courses on time management. On these, indeed on most management courses, I have yet to meet an executive who says that they have sufficient time. Yet on courses I run occasionally for groups of secretaries, they will all speak of the many things that their managers do that they could perfectly well cope with if allowed. On management programs, however, if it is suggested that more is delegated to secretaries there always seem to be reasons why not— *I am not sure they could really understand* . . . There is definitely a moral here.

So make sure that you really utilize your secretary's talents. A good secretary reflects well on the person (or people, secretaries are often shared) for whom she works and is able to help create an aura of efficiency about the office, and the activity in the office. Perhaps almost more important, she can be an ambassador for you, particularly in your absence, supporting decisions and policies, helping send out the informal messages that help create an image. And, of course, she can help make sure that work and projects are progressing as you would want (this is one of the reasons communication is so important; if she does not know your aims she cannot help achieve them).

A good secretary (and the same goes for PAs and assistants) increases your productivity, efficiency, and visibility. Never take her loyalty and assistance for granted and work at making her and her role a real asset to your work and career.

HELP OTHERS (AND REMEMBER TO SAY THANK YOU)

There is a danger that some of the suggestions of this section, keeping a people file, networking, and so on, may seem somewhat soulless and one-sided. This is not so and what you can achieve in these ways will be minimized if you see it like that. The simplest way of injecting a two-way element into these dealings is to remember to thank those who offer assistance, whether it is advice or something more tangible. For a start, this is just common courtesy. It is appreciated, and makes it more likely that those others involved will be disposed to help you again. A written note is often more appropriate than simply a word, especially when directed at the older generation.

Secondly, this kind of assistance is a two-way street. You will be more able to obtain the further assistance you need if you return any favors; indeed, not only is it useful to have the reputation for being a ready source of assistance for others, the whole process actually becomes more interesting and satisfying. In a busy life it is all too easy to lose touch, not get back to people, or otherwise put good networking relationships at risk. Sit back and think—to whom do you owe a thank you? After all, other people are the greatest asset to building a career after you. The implications of this continue, certainly in the next chapter when we turn to the importance of communication.

At the risk of repetition, it should be said that the influence of the people with whom you work, indeed with whom you cross paths in any way during your work, cannot be overestimated. Harvey Mackay, the American management guru, is quoted as saying: *If you want one year of prosperity, grow grain. If you want ten years of prosperity, grow a tree. If you want 100 years of prosperity, grow people*. It is a point well made, and the "people aspect" of the points made in this book pervades the whole process of career development.

In talking to people about their careers, I find that a particular person is always one of the first things they mention to explain any success. Sometimes that person is inherent to their career, a past line manager perhaps; sometimes it is some other contact, one seemingly made only by chance. But very often it is the action they took to develop a contact that was really what helped them. So it is not just the people contacts that can assist career development, it is what you make of them, whether that entails asking a single question or developing some kind of long-term association.

Always remember that you do not work in isolation—other people influence the path you take and you should influence them.

step **4**

THE POWER OF COMMUNICATIONS: MAKING IT WORK FOR YOU

"I guess I should warn you. If I turn out to be particularly clear, you've probably misunderstood what I've said."

DR ALAN GREENSPAN

Most of what goes on in the workplace is, in fact, communications; and anything that is not is probably dependent on some form of communications to initiate it or keep it going. If you work for an organization, then you are in communications. Your ability to communicate, and the way in which you do so, is so important to your career that here it is dealt with in its own chapter, though it is certainly one of a number of career and management skills which are dealt with elsewhere.

RECOGNIZE THE DIFFICULTIES OF COMMUNICATION

The first step to using good communications to further your career is to recognize the difficulties and resolve to work at avoiding them; more than that, to resolve to excel at communications. Consider this as a way into the topic:

As a busy manager you communicate all the time—verbally, in writing, with a variety of people—and do so perfectly well most of the time. Occasionally, however, you will find someone asking, "What do you mean?" in response to something that you have said. Sometimes you initiate the correction—"Sorry, I meant. . ."—and sometimes people will say to you: "You want me to do *what*?" As you can see, communication is not always as easy as it seems.

Communication can suffer from being unclear—*You fit the thing onto that sprocket thing and. . .* (just try it). Or imprecise—*and then it's about a mile* (three miles later. . .). It can be so full of jargon that we find ourselves referring to a manual excavation device, instead of calling a spade a spade. Or it can be incomprehensible "gobbledegook." Consider: *Considerable difficulty has been encountered in the selection of optimum materials and experimental methods but this problem is being attacked vigorously and we expect the development phase will proceed at a satisfactory rate.* (We are looking at the guidelines and trying to decide what to do.) There are innumerable barriers to communication, not least the assumptions, prejudices, and inattention of those on the receiving end.

All this may simply cause a bit of confusion, and take a moment to sort out, or it can cause major problems either immediately or later. Never are there more likely to be problems than when there is an intention to get someone to do something. Not only has the message got to be particularly clear but, because the days of saying, *Do this* to anyone in most organizations have long since gone, much communication needs to be *persuasive*.

If you are going to work with people and you are going to get things done, you need to communicate clearly and, very often, persuasively. What is more, you need to be seen to do so. Your communication breakdowns can cause problems for others, something that is hardly likely to mark you out as a high flyer. Your communications successes label you as competent, capable, and, on occasion, mark your abilities as excellent. They are disproportionately important because, as we shall see, others may well read excellence in communication as indicating a broader competency. And the need to persuade, getting your own way, particularly being able to obtain support for decisions and action that prove successful, is simply vital. Few careers progress without a strength in this area. The next sections examine the most important aspects of this fact.

COMMUNICATE CLEARLY

Crystal clarity should be the aim of all your communication. (It goes without saying, at least in this section, that if you are going to communicate you have to have something worth while to say— assuming that, whatever it is must be made clear.) The last section highlighted the inherent difficulty of successful communication. Here I want to help you think about making your messages clear and surmounting those difficulties. As luck would have it, prevailing standards are on your side because every office in the world tends to be witness to regular communications breakdown. Habit and prevailing style can compound the problem with "office gobbledegook," bureaucracy, jargon, and complexity dressed up as substance all combining to obscure any meaning that may lurk within the confusion.

You can probably think of examples in your own office, at meetings, in emails, or just in conversation over coffee where you come away saying: "What was all that about?" My favorite example is a much circulated office memo, all too probably based on fact. It is worth repeating here.

Standard Progress Report

For Those with No Progress to Report

During the survey period, which ends February 14, considerable progress has been made in the preliminary work directed toward the establishment of the initial activities. *[We are getting ready to start, but we have not done anything yet.]* The background information has been surveyed and the functional structure of the component parts of the cognizant organization has been clarified. *[We looked at the project and decided that George would lead it.]*

Considerable difficulty has been encountered in the selection of optimum approaches and methods but this problem is being attacked vigorously and we expect the development phase will proceed at a satisfactory rate. *[George is looking through the handbook.]* In order to prevent unnecessary duplication of previous efforts in the same field, it was necessary to establish a survey team, which has conducted a rather extensive tour through various departments with immediate access to the system. *[George and Harry had a nice time visiting everyone.]*

The steering committee held its regular meeting and considered rather important policy matters pertaining to the overall organizational levels of the line and staff responsibilities that devolve on the personnel associated with the specific assignments resulting from the broad functional specifications *[untranslateable—sorry]*. It is believed that the rate of progress will continue to accelerate as additional personnel are made available for the necessary discussions. *[We will get some work done as soon as we find somebody who knows something.]*

As a result of such shortfalls, things are delayed, communication takes up more time than it should, and, at worst, mistakes are made and things go wrong. The career-minded simply cannot afford to be like this, because the other thing that happens is that individuals are linked to and characterized by their communication style. If you are clear, really clear, then you stand out in this sea of confusion, and do so to your advantage.

Think of the impact of clarity: a clear succinct summary in a report or proposal: a complex sequence of events spelled out so that the key elements shine forth; a plan, policy, or procedure that all can understand first time—these are all noticeable to their recipients. Such things stand out because they make understanding easy for those to whom the communication is directed. If you can do this and do it consistently in your job, and get a reputation for so doing, it creates a powerful feeling of confidence in your abilities. A poor plan well explained is not as good as a good plan well explained, but both are likely to do better than a poor plan poorly explained. So, if you have to respond to recommendations designed to improve efficiency by rearranging the office layout, do not say: *Man—machine interface requirements in the system environment impose restrictive visual acuity problems on word-processing activity.* Rather say, *But it is arranged so that the secretary cannot see the VDU screen.* The following highlights key principles of clear communication; it is a task you must learn to undertake consistently well. So, to make your message clear:

- Choose an appropriate method (verbal, written—whatever)

- Be clear in your own mind what your objectives are in communicating

- Put your message in a form that suits the intended recipient(s). Anticipate and avoid misunderstandings, favor simplicity, be succinct, avoid jargon and unnecessary complexity

- Match what you put over to the experience of those addressed

- Aim to create and maintain interest (people will not understand if they do not listen properly)

- Choose the right time and avoid distractions

- Be practical (a total lack of realism may switch people right off)

- Watch for, and adjust to, reactions as you go

We are into some big issues here and the intention is not to provide definitive guidance to topics like communication, but key issues can be flagged. Next we consider the other side of communicating.

LISTEN (REALLY LISTEN)

Communication is a two-way street. It is important how you put any message over but it is also important how you respond. One key response to other people's communication is to listen. It is always a compliment to be described as a "good listener"; indeed, this is a good characteristic to cultivate as part of your career profile.

Listening, and being prepared to listen, makes an impression. And, of course, there is the immediate feedback that will help you to manage any conversation better. But there is listening, and there is listening. The trouble is that the mind can listen faster than people can speak—yes, literally. This means that the mind has time to wander as you listen (often getting ready what you are going to say next, especially if it is contradictory) and it does; so listening becomes inefficient. The result? The all-too-frequent "Sorry, what did you say?" which can signal not simply inattention, but also a lack of interest. This alone is sufficient to get two people at cross-purposes.

Clearly listening is vital, but it is not enough just to say that. You need to make listening another *active* process. This involves:

- Listening very carefully

- Concentrating on listening

- Taking note of what is said (mentally and/or writing notes)

- Appearing to be a good listener

Above all, adapting how you proceed in the light of the information other people give and, an important element of this, *being perceived to do so*. Few things will endear you to others quite so much as their marking you down as a good listener. If some of these are an influence on your career, better still. It is a factor that needs only a little thought and can quickly become a habit. The result is worth striving for as really listening gives you the edge in conversation and labels you as a sensitive communicator. And, as has been said, everything that builds your ability to be, and be seen to be, a good communicator is valuable in career terms.

SEEK AND WATCH FOR FEEDBACK

Listening, referred to above, is only one, albeit major, form of feedback in communication. You will only be a good communicator if you resolve to note and use all the signs given by others and work at doing so. This implies a number of things, including that you should:

- Watch for visible signs (gestures, expressions, etc.)

- Listen for non-verbal signs (things not said but sounded, such as a grunt of disapproval or a tut of impatience)

- Ask questions (itself a skill worth cultivating)

- Read between the lines—in speech as well as in writing—to see what may really be meant. As I am sure you have noticed, people do not always say what they mean; thus, a sentence that begins, *With the greatest respect*. . . is usually followed by an argument that respects the other party very little if at all

All this and more will put you in a better position to communicate more effectively (and more efficiently, because it will keep matters on track). Again it is a skill to be cultivated, part of the comprehensive overall ability you need as a communicator if you are to use this ability as a skill to further your career.

So far in this section, the points have been about communications generally. This is important enough, but there are several aspects, or particular forms, of communication that are especially important to the effectiveness of an individual in an organizational environment, and thus to their career prospects. We turn to these under the next few headings.

YOU MUST BE ABLE TO PRESENT "ON YOUR FEET"

There is an old saying: *The human brain is a wonderful thing. It starts working on the day you are born, goes on and on, and never stops until the day you must stand up and speak in public.* You may know the feeling; indeed, even the most experienced presenter may experience things like a dry mouth, shaking hands, "butterflies in the stomach," that can act to make this a traumatic experience.

There are so many circumstances in which the skills of formal presentation are needed, for example:

- Presenting to customers

- Dealings with suppliers and collaborators

- Internally (and often with senior people)

- Carrying out public relations activities (e.g. speaking at a conference)

There are a hundred and one different ways where plans, ideas, or developments are dependent on how something is put over and when it must be put over "on your feet." It is for most, if not all, people *simply not something you can avoid*. There can be only one response from anyone intent on career development: you have to learn to present and learn to do it well.

If you are not currently comfortable with this area, do not despair. It is a skill and it can be learned (I know: it is an area where I do a great deal of training and I have seen many people over the years amaze themselves with just what they can do—once they know how to go about it). What makes it easier? Preparation is the first thing, a clear structure—a beginning, a middle, and an end—is important, and there are a variety of tricks of the trade that will assist. A complete rundown on what makes for success is beyond the brief for this book. (I have written at length on the subject, see *The Management Speaker's Handbook* (How to Books).) But make no mistake: people tend not to say "What an excellent plan, what a pity it was not better presented"; they say "What a bad presentation, it cannot be much of a plan"—and the same principle is applied to the presenter. Thus not only is a good presenter more likely to get approval for whatever is presented, but also they are in all likelihood going to be seen as a step or two up in terms of overall competency than someone weak in this area.

The best way to improve these skills, having investigated them, is practice. It may well be that if you want to add the power of presentation to those skills that will help your career progress, you should actively seek out opportunities to make some or make more. Providing you think about it, the more you present, the more your technique for doing it will improve. Not only is it useful, but also there is a great deal of satisfaction to be had from making a presentation that is well executed and well received.

YOU MUST BE FLUENT IN WRITTEN COMMUNICATION

Writing is easy; all you do is sit staring at a blank sheet of paper until the drops of blood form on your forehead. This was said (by Gene Fowler) about creative writing, but it might come equally to mind as you contemplate that report you have to submit to the Board in two days' time. The message in this section is similar to that contained in the previous section on formal presentations. Most jobs come with paperwork—some of this is routine administration, some is very important.

Just like presentations, written communication—reports, proposals, even minutes and memos—can have a great deal hanging on them. Decisions that you want to go a particular way may be influenced not only by the quality of the thought, idea, or proposal, but also by how the case for it is made and how it is expressed in writing. Consider a report. Think of one you have had to read. If it is clear, well structured, and descriptive; if it had a clear introduction and a succinct summary that really ties together the key issues, then it makes much more impact on you. Never forget, with an eye on your career, that everything you write says something about the writer. Thus any report speaks volumes about the skill, knowledge, expertise, competency of the writer—and their influence. Yours must do the same.

Again, this is a skill that can be developed. In my own case, my career took a path that made certain kinds of writing very important, first with proposals and reports when I first went into consultancy, then later with books. Not only is there often much hanging on these things, but also they have a permanence that, say, a presentation has not. They stay around to haunt you and bosses are quite capable of producing for discussion at an appraisal meeting, a copy of a report written nine months or more previously. Anyway, in my case I saw the writing on the wall, as it were, and concluded it was something I had to work on and improve. I read about it, attended seminars, and, most important, became much more aware and critical of what I did. My style improved. I do not delude myself that I am the best writer in the world (and the great novel is still on Chapter One), but I can produce sufficiently workmanlike writing in a number of areas to earn part of my living from it. It is also a skill that you can spend a lifetime fine-tuning. So it should be with your business writing—regular work on it will improve it. And an effective and appropriate style will reflect well on you in your current job and in the view taken by other people regarding your future.

One form is worth special attention: the now ubiquitous email. There is a grave likelihood of these being dashed off. How many do you receive that are abbreviated to the point of shoddiness—or, worse, that do not make complete sense and must simply prompt a reply to seek clarification? Of course, sometimes they can be short and informal—but always make clarity your first consideration, and do not allow them to become less formal than the occasion, and recipient, demands.

A last point may provide an added incentive for you to work on your skills in this area. As your writing ability improves, you get to do it faster. This saves time and is a worthwhile objective in its own right. You have only to look at the quality of much of the paperwork that circulates around many an office to see that prevailing standards often leave something to be desired; so write right and you have another essential skill that can differentiate you and make you stand out.

YOUR COMMUNICATION MUST BE PERSUASIVE

With much business communication, it is not enough to be clear; there is a need to persuade. People with whom you must communicate up, down, and around the organization are not going to agree with you instantly and automatically just because you communicate well. They have their own point of view and this may include not doing anything or doing something quite different from what you are suggesting. Selling is part of most management jobs. It may not be called that, or even thought of as that, but that is what it is; any other word is perhaps a euphemism.

Now you may feel instinctively that you are not a salesperson and that this is something that you really do not need to be involved in to do your job. You may be right; but how about this: would you like to get your own way more often? Would you like less argument about things? Would you like to be seen more as a leader and initiator, someone who makes things happen rather than just follows? If the answer to any of these points is affirmative, then you need to be able to communicate persuasively. If, in writing the last few sentences, I am doing this it is, in part, because I am putting up a case for your doing so on the basis that it will help *you*. If I just said, "Do it, I think it is right," then this is less powerful. Selling—persuasive communication—demands an approach based on an understanding of the people or person to be persuaded, something that sounds pretty much common sense, but it is also something where common sense and the various techniques involved need coordinating and thus the techniques need investigating and learning before it can be successfully deployed. However you do it, there will be many occasions in your career where your progress will benefit from being able to communicate persuasively. Agreed?

YOU MUST BE AN EFFECTIVE NEGOTIATOR

This is another communication skill with a direct link to personal effectiveness and career. Negotiation overlaps with persuasiveness. It is to do not just with whether an idea will be accepted or agreed—that is the job of selling—but with *how* agreement will be arranged, what the terms and conditions are to be. Again there are so many applications internally and externally to the organization, again it is a body of knowledge and techniques skillfully deployed that make it possible, again it is something worth investigation and practice. The balance of arrangements that negotiation can settle is important to activities all the way up the management hierarchy; if you start as you mean to go on and become adept in this regard, it will stand you in good stead.

MEET WITH CONFIDENCE—AS A PARTICIPANT

It would be wrong to omit something about meetings in this section. Much communication in business is not one-on-one but involves the interactions of groups—the ubiquitous meeting. Sometimes it seems to most of us that we spend far too long in meetings that achieve far too little, a situation that gives rise to remarks such as: *the ideal meeting is two—with one absent*. On the other hand, whatever the topic of the meeting, those attending it are on show, especially if representatives of senior management are present. If, when called on to contribute, you are unprepared, tongue tied, incoherent or muddled, and indecisive then you not only fail to make whatever point you wanted to make, but you are also visibly tagged with an "indecisive" label, or whatever label seems appropriate to your performance.

So, if you are at a meeting (make sure incidentally that you should be; you do not want to be seen attending what others regard as time-wasting sessions that hamper your productivity, particularly if they are actually time-wasting), go prepared. Always read the last minutes, and any notes or papers circulated for discussion, in advance. No matter that others may not; you should. There will be issues that face you that you can only pronounce on with some thought beforehand and you cannot afford to be caught out for the lack of a moment's "homework."

Be careful not to come over as showing off, but remember the key points of effective meeting participation:

- Be prepared

- Listen carefully

- Make notes

- Keep comments succinct and to the point

- Deal through the Chair and respect the agenda and any meeting formalities

- Do not be crowded out; if you have a point to make, ensure you do so and do so assertively or persuasively as necessary

- Never resort to abuse, but be prepared to fight your corner on a rational businesslike basis to make your point

- Be open-minded and respect others' points of view (though you do not have to agree with them)

Politeness coupled with firmness, assertiveness rather than aggression—all these make for a good meeting. If you can become known as someone who brings common sense, sound thinking, and appropriate manner to a meeting, you will get asked to the right ones more often and your performance at them will contribute to your being seen in the right light. Never become unthinking in even a routine meeting—you are always on show and there may well always be something to gain from them.

MEET WITH CONFIDENCE—CHAIRING THE SESSION

You may well have noticed that however well or badly a meeting goes, its manner is usually a direct reflection of the style and manner of the Chair and if no one is in the chair, the whole thing is usually a muddle from beginning to end. You are not going to rise any great distance up most organizations without the ability not only to attend a meeting and perform impressively, but also to chair a meeting effectively.

For the Managing Director at least, position and authority will work in their favor to keep things going well in some respects. Down the line, it is perfectly possible to find yourself chairing a meeting where some of those attending are more senior and more experienced than you. So it is an area where, though practice of course helps, you have to make a good start. Therefore, chairing a meeting is another skill worth researching and learning to excel at.

For example, the Chair must:

- Be prepared (preferably more thoroughly than others attending)

- Set and keep to the agenda and keep time (an ability to run to time is especially impressive to others)

- Keep control, yet encourage discussion, let people have their say and comply with any rules

- Be able to field questions, arbitrate in debate, and referee in argument

- See, and deal with, both sides of the case

- Summarize clearly

- Arbitrate where necessary

- Prompt and record decisions and maintain a reasonable consensus

This is another communication skill that will stand you in good stead in a number of fields and circumstances. Resolve to be a good Chair, acquire the skills to be so, and use them fairly as chairing is not about riding roughshod over everyone by sheer weight. Apart from anything else, others will resent the roughshod approach. Get things done, but get people feeling these are good decisions sensibly arrived at and that they contributed to the process and they will be queuing up to attend your meetings!

ASK QUESTIONS

There is a danger that we think about communications as concerned only with how we communicate to pass information or instructions to others. But the ability to thrive and do your job successfully is dependent on knowledge and information and all you need of this will not be delivered on a plate. You have to ask. Sometimes you have to balance this with not becoming a nuisance to those you ask, but otherwise the rule is ask, ask, and ask some more. This should become a habit. Its value is cumulative and the effect is most often useful and the impression positive. Open questions (those that cannot be answered "yes" or "no") tend to work best at getting the most information promptly and easily because they prompt fuller answers and create a dialog.

Having asked, of course, you must listen and note anything you need to retain. Communication is two-way and abilities in all the specialist areas of communication dealt with here not only highlight the general importance, but also pick methodologies that are prime candidates for career enhancement. It really cannot be stated too strongly: if your communications skills are weak then your career prospects can all too easily be restricted. Even in technical areas where you may feel other specialist skills make up for deficiencies here, they may not be able to be hidden. So give attention to the way in which you communicate and also to the method in which you do it.

SELECT YOUR COMMUNICATION METHOD WISELY

Imagine someone calls you out of the blue. You have not seen them for a while and you invite them for a meal. You are pleased to see them, you lay on the arrangements rather specially, and a very good evening results. Then a few days later, you get either a call to say thank you or a specially written note. Which would make the better impression as a "thank you"? Most people would probably think that the letter was extra nice, taking more trouble than just lifting the telephone. Certainly, whatever view you take, they each make different impressions (and for many the email lags further behind).

So, any medium of communication has its own special effect. And there are a great many ways of communicating: one-to-one, a meeting, a memo or email, a letter, a circular, or a note on the company bulletin board. They work in different ways. Take email, perhaps the most modern form of universal communication. It speaks of urgency, but it can be less formal—people write in what is almost an internal memo style to contacts in other companies who they have never met and to whom they would be much more formal in a letter. Pick the methodology right and what you do will be thought appropriate; pick wrong and you are thought hasty, uncaring, or unthinking. What is the right way to communicate to someone that they are being fired? Or to a group that one member of the team is now in charge? Or to a senior manager so that they are most likely to give time to think about something? Each case and each person needs thought. Getting it right adds something positive to your image.

For some, with both the nerve and the influence to carry it off, a unique style can be added to certain communications. I know one manager who sends everything out on a letterhead printed in the color brown, he has brown ink in his laser printer to match, and also signs letters in matching brown ink. The net effect is classy and distinctive rather than pretentious. But add this kind of element with care. Getting the method right can add powerfully to what you communicate and what you communicate always says a great deal about you.

USE THE GRAPEVINE

The grapevine, or informal communications network, in an organization may take many forms. In one company in which I worked, it consisted almost entirely of the company tea lady, as she moved around and around the office during the day, so the news— good and bad, accurate and wild rumor—went with her. The tea lady just mentioned was not intent on doing this so much as primed by those who knew how things worked in this respect—anyone aware of the system could have a word with her when the first tea of the day came around in the morning, and know that everyone in the office that day would get the message by going-home time.

This is not really a digression and it does make a point. Unless you are plugged into the grapevine you may well miss a great deal. Worse, you may put yourself at a disadvantage, by not being aware when others are, of anything from policy changes to the imminent departure of key members of staff. Of course, you need to be able to read between the lines; not everything the grapevine has to say is true, though even the rumors may have a basis in fact and give you some advance information.

What action does this suggest? First, as I have said, that you should work out how the grapevine works and tap into it. Secondly, that you should use it—it is as useful as a channel to pass around what you want to say as it is a source of information. And finally, read, mark, and learn from what information it tells you, and use this as part of the image you present of someone well informed, with a finger on the pulse, which can help paint a positive image for you. One caution: if the grapevine is being used politically or maliciously, be very careful. It is one thing to be well informed; it is quite another to be marked down as the instigator of such gossip. That does no one's career any good.

THINK BEFORE YOU SPEAK

Or, as the old saying has it, *engage the brain before the mouth*. I suspect that many a career has been blighted by some ill-chosen remark or statement, and people left with the feeling that it is all too easy to say something in haste and find yourself repenting at leisure. The consequences of communication may be broad and many. Every time you open your mouth the image of how people see you is adjusted a little and you need to think not just of the context of a comment made but about what other results it may have. In part, this is a matter of manner. It is quite possible to disagree without actually saying, *That's garbage* and, in any case, many matters in business are better for some consideration.

There is rarely a problem in saying, "I don't know," or "I would like to think about that," or "Perhaps I could check." Certainly there is less chance of a problem occurring if you go down this road than if you proceed without due thought. If this all seems only like so much common sense, so it is. However, before passing on because you feel common sense is your stock in trade, consider for a moment some of the things that can make charging in more likely: anger, surprise, pressure (at being put on the spot), lack of preparation (perhaps prior to a meeting), dislike of the person or proposition with which you are dealing. All make an ill-considered outburst more likely; all make it less likely that such an outburst will match your considered view or be a well-directed piece of communication.

There are moments when biting your tongue and a little thought are great career developers.

GETTING THE MOST FROM JOB APPRAISALS

This is not the place for me to commend to organizations the merits of a good appraisal system, one that makes a constructive contribution to maintaining and improving performance standards, though it may be worth noting that in my experience you are likely to encounter different kinds of appraisal in a career that spans a number of different employers. Not all of them will be effective; some managers are bad at conducting such meetings, and you may not feel all are constructive. So be it. Careers do not progress in a perfect world, but any appraisal constitutes a major, and potentially career enhancing, form of communication and you should seek to get the most from them whatever they are like. The key issues are fourfold:

1. APPRAISALS: PREPARING FOR THEM

Be sure you understand how the appraisal system in your organization works before you find yourself in such a meeting. Incidentally, this is a good topic to investigate when you are being interviewed for a job, but before your first meeting you are likely to need more detailed information than is spelled out at that stage. First time around, ask for information if this is not provided and ask some of your longer-serving peers how their meetings go, how long they last, and what they get from them. Particularly be sure you know *why* appraisals are done, how management conducting them views them, what they look to get from them, and what time span the review covers.

Then you can consider how you want the meeting to go and how you can influence it. For instance, ask yourself what:

- *You* want to raise and discuss

- Is likely to be raised (and responses to any negative areas that may come up)

- Is the link between appraisal and the development and training you hope to receive

- Is the link between the meeting and your future work, responsibilities, and projects undertaken

If it is not your first appraisal, check what was said at, and documented after, the last one. This must be done in the context of what you now know about the forthcoming appraisal meeting. A couple of points are worth careful planning:

- One is the link to salary review and other benefits. Many organizations separate discussion of this from appraisal meetings (indeed there is a strong case for doing so); if this is the case it cannot be raised, except perhaps in general terms. If it will be discussed, you may have things to prepare here also

- Another is the make-up of the discussion in terms of time scale. A good appraisal will always spend more time on the future than on the past; both aspects need thought and certainly there is no excuse for your not having the facts at your fingertips about anything that is a likely candidate for discussion in the review of past events

Make notes as you plan, and take them with you to the meeting— there is no point in trusting to memory and, in any case, being seen to have thought seriously about the meeting will benefit you. You may only get one, sometimes two, such opportunities in any single year. Therefore, some careful preparation will prevent the occasion being wasted.

2. APPRAISALS: ATTENDING THEM

The person who is conducting the appraisal will have a bearing on both how it is done and how you need to conduct yourself. If it is with a manager with whom you are on good terms and see every day, this will make for a less formal meeting than if it is someone more senior with whom you only have occasional contact (numbers of appraisals involve three people including the person who is to be appraised).

A good appraisal will:

- Be notified well in advance

- Have clear agenda

- Have a particular duration in mind

And so these are things you should ask for if necessary. Particularly you may want to have ideas about how much time will be spent discussing last year and next, how interactive the meeting is, and when you can ask questions, perhaps also what is, and is not, on the record. Some appraisals are rather checklist in style; that is, the appraiser leads the conversation and raises the points one at a time, asking for your view or comment. Others are more open and allow the person being appraised to lead, pulling them back to an agenda only if the meeting digresses too much. Ideally you will know which way it runs, but you must be ready for either.

Remember lack of comment may be read as lack of awareness, knowledge, or as indecisiveness. On the other hand, if the question posed needs some thought then it is better to let the appraiser know rather than answering with a hasty comment.

Appraisals should not be traumatic occasions. If they are constructive—and prompting change in the future is the only real reason for doing them—then you can take a reasonably relaxed view of them (provided you have done some preparation) and there is no reason why you should not enjoy them as well as find them useful. You are on show, career-planning decisions are being made, albeit long term, by those conducting these meetings, but it is also a positive opportunity for you to present something of your competency in a way that goes "on the record."

3. APPRAISALS: THE FOLLOW-UP

Appraisals are too important just to file away in your mind or forget about once they are past. They can provide a catalyst to an ongoing dialog during the year. In many organizations, the system demands that the appraiser documents proceedings, and usually that the appraisee confirms that this documentation is a true record of the salient issues.

But there is no reason why you cannot take the initiative on particular matters. Consider the following as an example. Development requirements are one topic that most appraisals review. This may result in specific action—*I will enrol you on that communication course next month*—or it may result in further discussion, more than can be accommodated in the appraisal meeting itself. It may be useful to volunteer to undertake the processes involved (remember your boss could have a dozen appraisals in the same week and much attendant administration). If you put in a paper setting out some suggestions for action, and if this is used as the agenda for another session about it, then this could well see more of what you plan to happen happening, and happening sooner, than would otherwise be the case. Similarly use the opportunity to report back after any agreed training, in writing or at a meeting, so that the dialog continues. If the training has been agreed as successful then there is logic in discussing "what's next."

A final point—you may think attending them is a chore, but appraisals are not easy to conduct, take time to prepare, and always seem to be scheduled during busy periods. So, if your appaisal has been useful, express thanks and if it has not, try to comment in a way that may set the scene for a more productive encounter next time.

4. APPRAISALS: ACCEPT AND LEARN FROM CRITICISM

A good appraisal is likely to be a good meeting. Even if it is poorly conducted and not really very constructive, it is a satisfying feeling to come out saying to yourself, "I did well," particularly when someone else has told you so. But unless you believe the graffiti that says *I used to be great, but now I am absolutely perfect,* few of us get through many such meetings without having to take some criticism. We must consider the possibility that it is fair comment. You are probably not perfect, you do not get everything right and excel in all you do, and you sometimes get things wrong.

Because, perhaps understandably, no one likes having their failures, even minor ones, aired in public, there is a danger that you simply put such comment out of your mind and concentrate on the good things that are said (almost all appraisals will touch on both). Careers are not enhanced by either repeating mistakes or ignoring failings or weaknesses. If you do not take action after an appraisal and do so promptly, at least in terms of planning such action, then the moment will pass. Resolve to take note and, if necessary, action and you will do yourself and your career a favor.

Without a doubt the way you communicate is key to your effectiveness and to the likely success of your career development.

Way back in ancient Rome, Marcus Fabius Quintilian said: *One should not aim at being possible to understand, but at being impossible to misunderstand.* It is a sentiment we would all do well to take on board. The nature and quality of your communications, however they are manifested, are an inherent part of your corporate profile. Effective communication will help you succeed in your job and be seen as a professional, especially as some of the methodology discussed in this chapter involves issues where prevailing standards are not universally high. So making a good presentation, for instance, not only stresses your overall competency, it differentiates you from others, and does so positively.

Other skills are important too, as we see in the next chapter.

 *Every* time you communicate, you have an opportunity to influence your career, for good or ill.

step **5**

CAREER SKILLS: GIVING YOURSELF AN UNFAIR ADVANTAGE

"Hitch your wagon to a star; keep your nose to the grindstone; put your shoulder to the wheel; keep an ear to the ground; and watch the handwriting on the wall."

HERBERT PROCHNOW

Different jobs need different skills. I do not doubt that a wondrous grasp of the intricacies of regression analysis will help the statistician, almost as an ability to run fast might help a bank robber. However, here I want to review something of those skills that have common application in business and in management jobs rather than more specialist skills such as those just mentioned. The following are important in themselves and, the important thing here, are *career skills* of special importance in making career progress.

The first such skill is communications, which has already been the subject of comment in its own chapter. The other examples discussed here may well apply to you and your job. In the future no doubt, changes, currently difficult to predict, will necessitate your adding to the list. Certainly the rate of change is such these days that in an average career of, say, 40 years—age 20 through to 60—many things are hardly going to be the same throughout the time spanned.

GETTING AND STAYING UP TO SPEED

Given the complexity of jobs and the workplace, not getting out of date must be an unbreakable watchword. Some of this is with technical matters: as for an accountant having to keep up to date with tax matters, or almost everyone having to extend computer and IT skills. New skills may be necessary too as your job broadens. Resolve to keep matters under review and take action as and when necessary; more about this appears under development in the next chapter.

BE SUITABLY NUMERATE

Mathematics is not everyone's strong suit. But ultimately business is all about profit, and many jobs are involved directly with finance—whether revenue or cost—in one way or another. There are exceptions—non-profit-making organizations, charities, government departments, and so on, but, while profit may not be the driving force, finance still usually plays a key role, so a degree of numeracy is important in many jobs. Modern management education makes this a less likely gap than in the past. For some, the moral may be to avoid jobs with too much involvement; for others, certainly if you are going in the direction of general management, a certain minimal strength here is essential.

A "trainer's tale" illustrates this. On one particular course, one man could not get anything right in finance and he left the session very much the class dunce. The group planned to meet up in a year's time to see how everyone was faring, and in due course a dinner was scheduled in a smart hotel. The "dunce" arrived late, but it was clear to all from the Porsche parked in front of the hotel, the suit he wore, and a dozen other signs of affluence that he was doing very well for himself.

"I would never have thought it possible," said the tutor, "Tell us, what are you doing?"

"It wasn't easy," he replied, "I tried various things, but I finally ended up in the import/export business in Africa. I discovered that I could buy goods on one side of the border for $2 and sell them on the other for $4. It's just amazing how that 2 percent adds up."

The more numerate reader will recognize that this is not at all how percentages work, and for most of us such a gap in our expertise is unlikely to work out so well.

BE COMPUTER LITERATE

For some, computer literacy is already the norm. Others are currently either struggling or moving closer to some expertise in this area, a process that will never end as the technology moves on inexorably all the time. When this area is commented on, the advice is often to become keyboard literate as well. Until voice recognition takes some serious leaps forward, this is certainly sensible.

The so-called "IT revolution" is having a wide effect on many different aspects of business, not only within an organization, but also in terms of communication between organizations and with groups such as suppliers and customers. For example, some field salespeople are already carrying and using hand-held terminals to link them to their office, to record information, check stock, and input orders. In many stores computerized cash points not only record what has been sold and adjust stock level records, but in some cases the computer involved can also automatically reorder more stock direct from a supplier, computer to computer, with no other action involved. One could list a hundred examples, and in a year's time a hundred more.

Most people have to be knowledgable about what processes can be carried out by computers, many are going to have to work with the various forms of equipment involved, and some are going to have to anticipate how all of this will affect their organizations, their people, and their commercial prospects. Computers and this kind of technology do not automatically guarantee improvement in every area. There are many things they will not do, some at least they will never do, and some where, although technology has revolutionized the way something is done, it does not guarantee the right end result and in some organizations the statement, *It is in the computer* . . . has become synonymous with delay or inflexibility. The early computer saying about "garbage in and garbage out" still applies.

For all that, when push comes to shove, there are few people whose careers are looking ahead who will not benefit from increasing knowledge and operational ability in this exciting field. Meantime, I continue to set myself modest objectives and remain determined to get the better of the machine on which this book is being written; it has revolutionized my life, but there are occasions when it seems to have a mind of its own, jumbling
things
   up
   and
not **doing** as 58#.. IT IS TOLD *[sic]*. Worse to contemplate is that in fact it only does exactly as it is told, so any glitches are doubtless

my fault. Getting a real grip on whatever forms of technology we all have to use, or will have to use in the future, is important, and some thought within career plans about what you may need to be able to do and how you will achieve it is certainly worth while.

BE ASSERTIVE

Most if not all organizations are competitive arenas in which to work. It is also a fact of life that excellence in your area of expertise and in your job is not any guarantee of success. In most organizations, there is at least some conflict between departments, activities, and individuals.

To a considerable degree this is inevitable. Now make no mistake, this is not all bad. Friction and competitiveness can act to keep an organization on its toes. It ensures constant debate and may well have a constructive effect unless it becomes too extreme. In any event it is there. The question is what is the appropriate response to it? The career-minded have, I believe, to adopt an assertive attitude within their work and work environment.

There is, it should be noted, all the difference in the world between being assertive and being aggressive. If you are aggressive, and this may well go with—or be seen as going with—being unreasonable, self-seeking, unthinking, selfish, and more unflattering traits, this is unlikely to do your career much good. Though there are people who bludgeon their way to the top through their sheer aggression, this is not so common. Characteristics that better help include being determined and hard-working, having real ambition, and pushing for what you want.

Assertiveness is so often necessary in a variety of ways. When you put forward a point of view, a suggestion, or a plan, it must be put over with conviction. If you do not seem to present it with all the courage of your convictions, then why should others feel it is demanding of their attention and consideration? Assertiveness is at its most powerful when it is considered. That means to say that while sheer assertiveness will add some credibility to a point of view, if that point is not valid, not well thought out, or ill conceived, then there is no great likelihood of it carrying the day. There is no guarantee that a sound argument will carry the day either, but put over energetically—with some assertion—then it will stand the best chance of acceptance.

This principle must become a habit. Its application would range from how one point is emphasized in a conversation, to the preparation of an annual plan or appraisal meeting so that holding back becomes a considered opinion. However, your normal mode of communication, while tailored to the different kinds of people with whom you interact, should always do justice to the points you wish to make.

Successful careers are built on success. You first have to achieve that success before you can benefit from how it positions you within your organization. Analyze how you come over presently; perhaps you should sometimes consider being just a little more assertive. No, I will restate that—be more assertive where necessary!

MASTER DECISION MAKING

Decision making is important in the context of this book in two separate ways. First, the quality of the decisions you make in your job will directly affect your effectiveness and success, and, as is expressed in various ways throughout this book, this, in turn, affects your career. Secondly, you have to make decisions throughout your career about your career and exactly how you can best do this is worth examining in some detail.

To a degree there are no "right" answers in business, but there are certainly wrong ones. Experience is a vital factor in guiding us to pick the right alternative, though too much reliance on it can give a false sense of security and may stifle creativity. A procedure that is logical and systematic and that ensures due consideration of the alternatives, while not being infallible, will certainly help make more of your decisions, in a career context or otherwise, turn out right. This is the subject of another book in this series (*Think on Your Feet* by Jeremy Kourdi) so here I will only encapsulate core decision-making approaches in what is a neatly ten-step approach:

STEP 1: SETTING OBJECTIVES

Before any action can be considered, the objectives of the exercise must be set. Unless you know where you are going, you cannot plan how to get there or how to measure your progress. For the objective to be valuable, it must be as specific and as quantitative as possible. Goals such as "increasing sales," "improving customer service," and "reducing costs" are useless, as they provide no basis for measurement. If the aim is to increase sales, it should be specified by how much and within what time period.

STEP 2: EVALUATING THE OBJECTIVE AGAINST OTHER COMPANY OBJECTIVES

When a clear, precise goal has been established, it should be compared with other company aims to ensure compatibility. Failure to do this is common, particularly in large companies. This results in different sections of the organization working toward objectives which in themselves are reasonable but which, when put together, become mutually exclusive; for example, the sales office manager may be trying to maintain business with small accounts, whereas marketing or sales management are planning to service them exclusively via wholesalers.

STEP 3: COLLECTING INFORMATION

Information can now be collected from which plans can be developed. It is unwise to start this data collection stage until clear, compatible objectives have been defined, otherwise vast quantities of useless figures will be assembled "for information" or "in case we need them." The advance of research techniques and the progressive development of the computer have stimulated the hunger for information. It is a great temptation to call for information simply because we know it is available. Mountains of figures may give a sense of security, but information is costly to process and is only useful (and economic) when it contains answers to precise questions, which have direct bearing on the decisions it is possible to take.

STEP 4: ANALYZING THE INFORMATION
It is the objective that will guide you toward the questions to be answered and thus the information needed. The lines of analysis to be followed will in turn be indicated by such questions. For example, declining sales in one area of the country, perhaps owing to the larger customers buying from competitors, should not prompt us to ask for *everything we know about the market*. What we really need is sales in that region broken down by customer type, possibly compared with similar figures for another area. From this analysis, we can proceed progressively through the relevant information, very much more precisely (and probably more quickly and economically) than starting with a dozen different breakdowns that attempt to show *all about everything*.

STEP 5: DEVELOPING ALTERNATIVES
The whole basis of this method of approach is to encourage us to think more broadly and creatively about possible solutions to problems. Sometimes, of course, the solution will become obvious from systematic processing of the data. In the majority of instances, however, no clear-cut answers will be found; a number of factors suggest themselves, or the answer lies in a combination of a number of factors.

STEP 6: CHOOSING THE "BEST" ALTERNATIVE
This is the heart of the decision-making process. It is unlikely that all possible solutions can be implemented; one must be chosen. To help in this choice, consideration should be made of four criteria:

- Cost
- Time
- Risk
- Resources

The costs of each alternative can be calculated and considered alongside the objective. Assuming that several approaches appear to be capable of achieving the objective, this might only narrow the choice. So the other yardsticks should also be used. Time taken might be a critical factor, or the element of risk (particularly of failure) or lack of certain resources might rule out other options; for example, a critical staff situation in an office may preclude certain courses of action.

The choice of the "best" alternative is then based on a consideration of all the advantages and disadvantages of all the possible alternatives. It is at this stage that experience can be particularly valuable. Its possible limiting effect will already have been overcome by the systematic search for alternatives.

Having made the choice, at least we will be well aware of what has been done in terms of the possible drawbacks of the decision and the discarded alternatives. It will also be easier at some time in the future to look back and assess why such a decision was, in fact, made.

STEP 7: COMMUNICATING THE DECISION

This is a step too often omitted. And yet unless all concerned know what is being done, impact will be lost. For example, it is commonplace to find inside sales staff whose first knowledge of an advertising campaign is gained from customers. In such circumstances, communication must be systematically planned.

Information may well have to be passed by different methods and in different forms to different people, in writing, by telephone, meetings, and so on. By communicating only necessary information by the most appropriate methods, far better results will be gained than by a blanket memorandum with copies to everybody.

STEP 8: SETTING UP THE CONTROL SYSTEM

Remember that this stage occurs before implementation. This is because in many cases the process of implementing a plan destroys the ability to evaluate it. For example, in a situation where it is believed that staff lack some necessary knowledge, the decision might be taken to run a training program. At the end of the course a test is given in which the average score is 90 percent. It might be concluded, therefore, that the program was successful. But, as there has been no measurement of what the test score would have been at the beginning of the program, it can never then be known whether it was successful or not.

STEP 9: IMPLEMENTING THE DECISION

Putting the decision into action should now be easy. It will have been clearly stated what is to be done toward what objective and why that particular action has been chosen, all concerned will have been informed, and the system of evaluation will have been set.

Research has shown that if change is to be implemented, then specific tasks should be allocated to particular people and deadlines laid down for the tasks to be completed. Vague requests for action can easily result in failure.

STEP 10: EVALUATING THE DECISION

Again assuming quantitative objectives, clear decisions, and predefined control systems, evaluation is simple. The problems of control and evaluation in management are caused by lack of clear yardsticks against which to compare. If you simply set broad qualitative goals of increasing, say, productivity *as much as possible*, you will have the utmost difficulty in evaluating the results. Without a marker, there will usually be no common definition of what constitutes an increase or an improvement.

DEVELOP A CREATIVE APPROACH

Words like "creativity" and "innovation" invoke what sound like highly desirable attributes of both organizations and people. They also conjure up typecast images of the creative department in an advertising agency or the innovation inherent as a high-tech company exploits latest developments. Ideas come in all shapes and sizes: they can be revolutionary or may be better characterized as evolutionary, the gradual process of change and development by which so much that drives an organization is carried forward. Most jobs involve some of this process, certain specialist areas consist mostly of this, and, generally speaking, senior people tend to have need of the highest skills in this area.

It may be sensible in dealing with such broad concepts to define our terms. Essentially, creativity is the thinking process that helps us generate ideas, whereas innovation is the practical application of such ideas toward meeting the organization's objectives in a more effective way. Innovation is thus the essence of corporate success, taking ideas and converting them into practical and workable ways forward. This being the case, individuals who have innovative and creative ways of approaching things tend to be favored in choices affecting who rises through the ranks of an organization. Clearly it follows that if you can develop this side of your abilities this may be something else favorable to your career.

Some faced with these comments abdicate all thoughts of success: *I am just not a creative person*, they say, as if it were something you are born with like brown eyes or perfect pitch. Maybe; but there is another view that says you can work at it. Consider an analogy. When someone writes a novel or a film script, something that in a different context would be regarded as a creative act, they need ideas. But they need other things as well: a process is involved that is to some degree structured. A story needs a beginning, a middle, and an end. If it is dramatic, each part will end with a cliff-hanger or reversal, with the next section turning things around and taking the plot forward. There are a mass of principles about what makes a character, say, sympathetic and all this goes with the ideas that must be built in to create the whole. Much innovation is not, in fact, creative in the sense of the wonderful new idea just popping ready made into someone's head. It is hard graft. It is the systematic working at something in the right way that produces results.

Perhaps producing results is the key. You may never be sufficiently creative to write a sonata that will still be well thought of in a hundred years' time, but you may well have to produce results for your organization that cannot be done without some original thinking. This you can work at; after all, it is not so much creativity that is the key—it is *creating*.

TAKE A BROAD VIEW

One of the things that undoubtedly differentiate, management from direction (though not every director from every manager) is their ability to see—and take—the broad view. Again some will claim this is an inherent skill, others that it is something that can be developed. By broad I mean both in canvas and in time. An ability to do this is a characteristic shared by many entrepreneurs, or the more successful of them. An initial idea or premise gives rise to a vision of where that can take them, the kind of organization that can be built on it, the way it will work to create success, and what it will bring in terms of rewards.

Someone has to handle the details as well, of course, but most jobs benefit from taking the broad view and anyone who can stand back, particularly from immediate concerns or problems, and get things in perspective is likely to increase their effectiveness. Sometimes achieving this only means curbing the natural tendency to "jump in." This can show itself in both positive and negative situations: if someone says, "What can we do to solve this?" the temptation is to focus hard up front on the problem and possible solutions, but they may come more readily if the problem is seen in context: why is this occurring? What are we trying to achieve? Similarly with opportunities: ask, "What can we make of this?"

The best response may be to consider hard whether making anything of it will fit in with the overall activity, rather than instantly suggesting three or four development possibilities. The same principle of thinking should span activities. General management must always think about finance, resources, people and the market, and a dozen external factors, and more, always with the precise combination of factors matching the subject of consideration.

You may have such skills already, or have them in embryo form. If so, cultivate them, consciously take a broad view even of matters within a smaller scale in your own part of an organization; if not, start to develop them, particularly if you have a directing role in mind for yourself.

There is a link here to time. Those who take the broad view are usually those who take a moment to think about things. In a world where the pace of activity seems to increase daily, we all too easily fall into the habit of seeing everything as needing an instant response. Sometimes this approach can fail to achieve the best result.

I remember being asked a question by someone attending a course I was conducting. I began to set out what seemed to me a good way of resolving the issue and was met with a blank look. After a moment, I realized that the person who had posed the question, and had done so because they had thought about the issue and failed to come up with a solution, had only considered what might be called "quick fixes." It seemed to me that only sustained action over a period of time would fix things—a campaign, if you like—and, once they accepted that no quick fix was possible, they quickly became more creative in seeking a solution. This kind of realism is valuable, not only for solving problems, but also for career development.

Leaving the broad view to one side, these are not the only skills that might be described as career skills. Some others are reviewed elsewhere: communications in Step 4, time management in Step 7 (see page 122). You may need to think of others that are relevant to you in your field of work; these might range from learning to speak a second language to juggling with flaming torches without burning holes in the carpet—whatever they are you need to view them the right way and ensure that you take steps to arm yourself with the weaponry, as it were, of career development, which leads us logically to training and development.

 Identify the career skills you need, now and in the future, and work on developing them to a level where they act to enhance your career.

ENHANCING YOUR STRENGTHS: TRAINING AND DEVELOPMENT AS AN AID TO JOB PERFORMANCE AND CAREER SUCCESS

"Companies can't promise jobs for life, but by constant training and education we may be able to guarantee lifetime employability."

JACK WELSH

In recent years, more people in business are more and more well qualified. A degree, or more specifically a business degree, is regarded as the basic by many organizations. But having such a qualification is no longer sufficient—education in business should have a practical bias. It was once said, probably by someone less than well qualified, that the perfect business enterprise was to set up a trading house that purchased MBAs for what they were worth and sold them for what they *thought* they were worth! The point being that the arrogance of the MBAs would ensure a significant profit. By and large those with such qualifications are also practical these days (though the fact of having some such qualifications is no guarantee of this), but whatever the prime qualification it should be a beginning and not an end. Here we look at a number of career-building factors to do with development and consider how the right view of, and practice of, development can assist you.

ASSESS YOUR DEVELOPMENT NEEDS

To say you are actively developing your career in terms of training and everything that word implies, does not mean grabbing at every opportunity to, say, attend a course regardless of any consideration except that it is possible. You need to consider what development is necessary (which in job terms is what will happen through many organizations' job appraisal schemes). It is worth thinking this through in a systematic way and, of course, doing so honestly. Otherwise, your career will certainly suffer if you deceive yourself and ignore gaps in your knowledge or skills the filling of which would carry you forward.

First, you should remember that development can only do three things:

1. Improve your knowledge.

2. Develop your skills.

3. Change your attitudes.

With that in mind, consider the thinking involved in an ongoing systematic skills review, described here as a ten-step process:

Step 1: Identify the requirements of your present job in terms of knowledge, skills, and attitudes—you need to be honest about this and think broadly about it (and it is clearly easier if you have a clear job description).

Step 2: Identify your own current level of such knowledge, skills, and attitudes—look at how well you can perform in the job now.

Step 3: Identify any additional factors indicated as necessary in future because of likely or planned changes—in today's dynamic business climate there are likely to be some of these.

Step 4: Consider and add any additional aspects that your own longer-term career plan demands—this can look as far ahead as you wish, but realistically should concentrate on the short/medium term.

Step 5: Set priorities—note what needs to be done; there may well be more than it is realistic to change very quickly and you then need to set clear priorities to help you make progress.

Step 6: Set clear objectives—always be absolutely clear what you are trying to do and why.

Step 7: Consider the timing—in other words, when any development might take place, and this no doubt in a busy life means one thing at a time and perhaps at a slower pace than you would ideally like.

Step 8: Implement—do whatever is necessary to complete the development involved. This could be very simple: you doing something that you can control. Or it could involve discussion and debate with others to get agreement about the need and to committing the necessary time and money (for instance, to attend a course).

Step 9: Evaluate—this is an important one. Many people forget to really think through how useful and relevant something, like attending a course, is when a little review can ensure much better linking to the real job and future tasks.

Step 10: Assess against the job/career factors—as well as evaluating general usefulness of anything done, you need to match its effect with both current tasks and future career plans to see how well it helps with your specific work and plans.

Then you are back to the beginning again. The process is a continuous cycle, something where regular review is necessary, if not month by month then certainly year by year. Next you need to relate this to a plan and then think about the actions that are implied to see it through. We turn to some of these next.

HAVE A SELF-DEVELOPMENT PLAN

In today's dynamic world, development must be a continuous process. There will be new skills you need to acquire during your career and perennial skills to be kept up to date. If you are with an organization that has a sound development policy, the thinking needed here may well be prompted by what action is forthcoming from such activity. If not, or if what is done is, in your view and for your needs, inadequate, then you will need to initiate what happens here. You need a plan. Not something cast in tablets of stone that stretches into the future and is unchangeable, but a rolling plan, something that sets out immediate actions or intentions clearly and an outline for the longer term. The detail of this will have to change as events unfold, and you must adjust to changing circumstances and needs. Some such changes are fairly long term. In my own case, learning to type did not feature on my development plan for many years; then the amount of written work I did increased. It made sense to learn, so it went on the plan. Now the (permanent) objective is to do it more accurately and faster!

Other changes may be more rapid, and still affect your development intentions. A move to an overseas office, perhaps, or the organization setting up an overseas subsidiary, might prompt thoughts about language skills. The options in terms of action are several:

- The organization may suggest something (e.g. attendance on a course)

- You may want to suggest something to them

- You, or they, may want to amend or adapt an original suggestion

- You may conclude that, whatever the company does, you will do more to meet your personal objectives, including working in your own time

The permutations are, of course, many. The key thing is that you regularly devote a little time to considering what you feel would help. This means looking at immediate job advantages alongside long-term career ones (after all, the company will be more inclined to spend money on things that have a reasonably short-term impact for them, while you may want to look further ahead) and keeping your personal plan—which should be in writing—up to date.

There is an important link here with any company appraisal scheme that you find yourself taking part in—many organizations have their own schemes. Some consist of just an informal annual meeting. Others are more formal and more regular. Such schemes, if they are good, are very much to be commended (and are dealt with on page 78). Whatever kind of scheme there is, it is likely that you will find it includes a review of development needs. This is the moment to link your personal plan with that of the organization for which you work. With the support and approval of your immediate boss, you will probably find you can do more that will benefit your current job and the tasks it entails, and help yourself in the longer term as well.

Just as you need a career plan, you need a development plan. All business literature commends, indeed advocates, planning. This is not just because it is a formality that the academic texts insist on; it really works. If you take a moment to keep your thoughts straight about this area, you will be more able to action more of what you want and better able also to take advantage of circumstances.

A final point: some development is interesting, some may even be fun, and that is all well and good, but it does not mean it all will be. Some of the most useful developmental activities may be a very great chore. For example, to return to my earlier example, the typing course I went on was no fun at all; it was tiring, boring, and definitely a chore. But it was very useful. My typing may not be peRficT but it is good enough to have changed my work pattern in useful and productive ways. You may not know what skills or knowledge will change your own work pattern in future—but beware of putting off acquiring new skills because the process of doing so is a chore.

READ A BUSINESS BOOK, REGULARLY

As I make my living, in part, by writing this may seem like a plug, but reading a business book is certainly among the simplest forms of development and a good deal can be learned from it. It takes some time, but is also something that you can allocate to certain moments when perhaps time would otherwise be wasted. Such time includes traveling; and I know more than one salesman who always carries a business book to read in those, sometimes long, moments he regularly spends in his customers' reception areas.

The first rule is to make it a habit. Always have such a book on the go (even if it takes you a while to get to the end) and keep watching for what is current in bookstores, by reading the reviews in the press and getting yourself added to publishers' mailing lists.

There are two different kinds of book to concentrate on.

The first consists of those titles that link directly to your development need, like *How to Write a Better Report* or whatever. Your choice here may reflect immediate needs or something you wish to develop further ahead. Remember, it may be useful to come at things in different ways; the constructive repetition involved will help you take in the message, so it is worth reading more than one title on certain topics.

The second category consists of those books that are sufficiently popular (and useful—though the two do not always go together!) that you need to be seen to be up to date with them. Such a book (though any example will date) is something like the bestseller *The Tipping Point* (written by Malcolm Gladwell). Not strictly a business book, its title has entered the language and having a familiarity with it may be both useful and put out the right signals.

There is a danger in such circumstances that you will be perceived as not up to date if you are not familiar with such titles, though this should not be taken to extremes; if all your conversation becomes hung around quotes from such books people may think you do not have an original thought in your head.

This may seem a small point, but applied conscientiously its effect may be considerable. A book every quarter, for instance, is still quite an input of information over, say, five years of your career. Six a year is better still. You can apply the same principle to a range of things from technical journals to websites.

ATTEND A COURSE

Courses, seminars, workshops—whatever word you use, attendance on these events can be very beneficial. And in the long run a couple of days spent on such an event is not too high a price to pay compared to what may be gained from them. Some employers will regularly give you the opportunity to attend both external courses and those set up and run only for their personnel; if not you may want to prompt them. If you are making such suggestions, particularly to attend outside events, remember you must put your case persuasively. Just ask to attend and some of the thoughts that come to mind will be negative: *They want my job—once they have extended their skills a little more they will be likely to leave the organization.* So, tell them what *they* will get. Explain what more you will be able to do for them and for the organization; will you be more effective, more productive, able to save or make money? If so, explain.

Choose carefully. If you make wild suggestions, something that clearly only benefits you in the long term, or ask to attend something every week, you are unlikely to get agreement. Make practical suggestions and get approval and you perhaps create the right kind of precedent and habit. I remember once battling for three years for the budget and time to attend an annual conference in America. Once I had attended and it proved useful, then it rapidly moved to being a regular event. Certainly the most important consideration is the course topic and content, but realistically there are other things to think about: who is organizing it, speaking at it, and attending it? The style of events is important also; I am not alone, for example, in finding some of the best-known "gurus" disappointing in the flesh. You may want something with an international flavor or with specific relevance to your own industry or activity.

One single new idea, or even one single existing idea confirmed with sufficient weight to prompt you into action in some particular area, is all that is necessary to make this process worth while and at best there is a great deal to be gained by it. Under the next three headings we investigate specific aspects of course attendance.

CONDUCT YOURSELF RIGHT AT COURSES

It is said that you only get out of something what you put in. Certainly this is true of course attendance. First, once attendance is fixed, you should think through what you want to get from it. This will help you and the course tutor—I know my heart sinks if I ask people on seminars, that I conduct, why they are present and their only answer amounts to, "I was told to be here." Never go to a seminar without a written note of your objectives and any specific questions you want to obtain comments on. Most trainers are happy to get a note of questions in advance, though in my experience this is rarely done.

Thereafter you need to think about how you will behave "on the day." If the program is internal (in-company), you may know all the other participants and the whole tenor of the event may be informal. If it is external, it can be a little daunting to arrive in a room of participants none of whom you know. Everyone is in the same situation, however, and the informal contacts and the comments and shared experience of your fellow participants may be an important part of your attendance. The checklist that follows sets out the suggestions I often issue to course participants and makes, I think, some useful points about being open-minded and adopting an approach that is constructive. In view of the time and cost of attending such events, it is a great pity to walk away at the end with some key question still unanswered.

> **NOTES FOR DELEGATES: an example of a document issued to delegates at the start of a course (or ahead of attendance)**
>
> 1. This manual contains all the basic details of this training program. Further papers will be distributed progressively during the course so that a complete record will be available by the last session.
>
> 2. This is *your* seminar, and represents a chance to say what you think—so please do say it. Everyone can learn from the comments of others and the discussion they prompt.
>
> 3. Exchange of experience is as valuable as the formal lectures—but you need to *listen carefully* and try to understand other points of view if this is to work.
>
> 4. Do support your views with facts in discussion; use examples and stick to the point.
>
> 5. Keep questions and comments succinct—do not monopolize the proceedings, but let others have a say so that various viewpoints can be discussed.
>
> 6. Make points in context as they arise. Remember that participation is an attitude of mind. It includes listening as

well as speaking, but also certainly includes constructive disagreement where appropriate.

7. Make notes as the meeting progresses. There is notepaper provided in this binder. Formal notes will provide an *aide-memoire* of the content and coverage, so any additional notes should primarily link to your job and to action on your return to work. Even a few action points noted per session can act as a catalyst and help ensure action follows attendance.

8. A meeting with colleagues, staff, or your manager on your return to normal working can be valuable; it acts as a bridge between ideas discussed here and action in the workplace and can make change more likely.

9. It will help everyone present if you wear your name badge, respect the timetable, and keep cellphones and pagers switched off during the sessions.

10. This is an opportunity to step back from day-to-day operations and consider issues that can help make your job more effective. Be skeptical of your own operation, challenge ideas, remain open-minded throughout, and actively seek new thinking that can help you prompt change and improve performance.

NOTE: here also you may find listed any "house rules," the observance of which can improve the course experience for everyone attending.

It is important to adopt the right approach. Time on such an event goes all too quickly and it is easy to leave and then wish you had asked something else. Try not to worry about what people will think. Sometimes you may feel others are all ahead of you in understanding. Often they are not and a question postponed, because it seemed obvious and likely to make you appear stupid, actually, once asked, can prove to be a common question, which leads into very useful discussion for all.

MAXIMIZE COURSE ATTENDANCE BENEFITS

The most important thing about any course you may attend is what happens after it is finished. Courses may be interesting, they may even be fun, but what really matters at the end of the day is the action that they prompt. So, even more important than the notes you make before attending is the action plan you make afterward.

Noting such a plan has to start at once. It is inevitable for most people that, if you are away for even a couple of days at a short course, you are going to have more in the in-tray on your desk afterward than if you had not attended. Yet the moment to start any action resulting from the course is the following day. Nothing later will do, the likelihood is that you will get involved in catching up, and everything will be put on one side and forgotten.

So, whatever else you do, take ten minutes on the day after attendance to list—in writing—the areas of action you noted during the program. At least get them on your "to do" list whether they are things to think about, to review further, or to take action; whether they represent things you can implement solo or things you will need support or permission for and must raise at the next appropriate meeting. If you do this much and then approach them systematically and with an eye on the priorities, something is more likely to happen. If you miss this stage, the danger is not that you will do less, but that you will do nothing.

So, follow up your notes, do not just have good intentions but make firm action plans and consider also:

● Reviewing and keeping safe any course notes that were useful

● Having a de-briefing session with your boss, the training manager, or whoever sent you. If they are convinced it was useful, then future requests may be that much easier to make and get agreed. When this is done is worth considering. There cannot be much implemented action to report immediately after attendance, but your recall of the detail will be greater. Later on, you can review what you have done as a result more realistically. Thus two meetings may be worth while. If your company asks you to complete an assessment form about the course attended, always do so thoroughly and on time; they are useful to the process of deciding what training is used in the future. Not doing this may be seen as indicating you have no interest in training

- Filing away details of the course (and maybe the certificate of attendance) and add it to a list you can keep with your C.V. This is worth while as the memory fails quickly. Five years on when someone asks what you know about X, it may be useful to look up exactly when you attended a course on the topic and what it covered

Just attending a developmental event is nearly always useful. If it is a well-chosen and practical one then it may be very useful; and if you go into the process with the right attitude and take the right action before, during, and after the event, you will maximize the benefit that comes from it.

TAKE A DEVELOPMENT SABBATICAL

By this I mean taking time away from work to do some additional and longer course or activity. A post-graduate business diploma may be both a useful qualification to add to your C.V. and you may learn a great deal in doing it; so too with many types of project. But the pursuing of such projects may be sufficiently disruptive to a career to cause pause for thought.

Consider how you could go about this. Either your employer must sponsor you, accept you will be away for six months, a year or more, and perhaps finance this, at least in part, or you are going to have to stop work for a while and sustain yourself during the time such a course takes. The first is a major expense for the employer, one that they will need some persuading to undertake, and are realistically unlikely to do so unless they view your potential value to them very highly; do not ask for such an arrangement lightly or on your first day at work! Some may do no more than promise to consider rehiring you after the course is finished. The latter, of course, is expensive and difficult for you.

The other factor to consider is the time taken. You must balance how your career might progress in, say, a year with your current job and employer against what might be possible after taking a year out to attend some developmental project. But people certainly do it, and I have known those who undertook considerable sacrifice to save the necessary money and organize family affairs so that they could do a particular course. Usually the choice of institution attended is a prestigious one in order to maximize the career-enhancing effect of the new qualification in due course. Sometimes this means somewhere overseas, and this may be especially worth while for some, though it clearly increases the cost.

A final point here: age is no real barrier. I have known people take an additional period, a year perhaps (more in some cases) in their twenties or thirties. I have even heard of some who took early retirement, undertook extensive new training, and then set out to start a new career in a new field. Whether anything like this is worth considering depends on the qualifications you already have, what you want to do next from a work point of view, the sheer ability to organize job, family, and more to make it possible—and your own commitment to seeing it through. It is not for everyone, so proceed carefully.

The most manageable such thing is probably getting yourself seconded to some project internally on which you know you will expand your experience usefully.

CONTINUE LEARNING—AT A DISTANCE

Change, including technological change, affects almost everything in our lives, including education and training. One comparatively recent development in this area is the advent of what is called "distance learning." This is a rather imprecise term that covers a range of rather different things, but the principle in all cases is similar—that of receiving some kind of formal training (including education resulting in a qualification) by working alone linked to, but not actually attending, the establishment providing the tuition. These days this will often involve working online on the internet.

The options are many and varied and allow you to study part time while continuing to work full time and develop your career on the job front. You can undertake anything from an MBA to a short course covering some individual skill area. The form of the course will include conventional study, with things to read, but may also involve a series of other methodologies: videos, exercises, programmed learning, and, in the best formats, the ability to complete projects and papers that are sent away and then receive individual critique and comment to help you through the whole exercise. Some courses do involve some group activity, weekend sessions are sometimes used to fit this aspect in without making it impossible for those working full time to attend.

The area is worthy of some investigation for anyone wishing to extend their learning. But, a word of caution—because of the profusion of material that has become available there is, among excellent material and schemes, some that is frankly not so good. A good deal of work is involved in any lengthy distance learning course so it is worth selecting what you do carefully, and there are also considerable differences in costs.

Like anything you may do to bolster your learning there is a perception involved. The course may be good; you learn something that will benefit your career. In addition, the fact of your doing it, and the commitment clearly implied, makes a point to people and this too may count on your overall record. There are some institutions and providers that are more likely to make this kind of impact than others. So the total basis of choice must allow all these factors.

TAKE ON NEW THINGS

Make a point of taking on new things. Experience and the range of your competency are both things that must be kept moving, like sharks, which must keep swimming or sink. There is a temptation in many jobs to stick with the areas of work that you feel are "safe," by which I mean where you do not have to stretch and where you are sure of what you can do. This is almost always a mistake. Allowing that if you spread your learning too wide you may end up with some expertise across too broad a front rather than a real strength in particular areas, an ongoing objective to broaden your range of skills, expertise, and experience is likely to be helpful to you in the long run. As the American novelist Henry James said, "Experience is never limited, and it is never complete." Not only is the potential for broadening yourself vast, but so also are the possibilities of something added to your range of abilities acting to make a positive career change.

You never know what the future holds and, at the risk of my sounding very old, it is an easy mistake when young to rule out possibilities on the grounds of some inherent prescience. I know from my own experience that skills that have helped me more recently in my career formed no part of my expertise early on and, with hindsight, I do not think I always predicted what would be useful in this sort of way. So, next time something new is on offer, something that will stretch your powers and even where the outcome is somewhat more certain, think very carefully before you decide to avoid it or say *no*. You could be taking on something that will kick-start your career into its next move forward.

Development in all its manifestations is an inherent part of success in the organizational world. Once it was seen as an unfortunate chore; now "life-long learning" is accepted as a necessity for all. Management want people to have the right attitude to training. In the past, many managers said: *Training is to be avoided, it costs time and money*. Today, training is much more widely accepted, but if a manager now says, as some still do, that it might be a waste of resources (*What happens if I spend time and money on training, and people leave?*), the only possible answer is: *What happens if you don't train them, and they stay?* Ongoing development will help you; so will being seen to do it.

Development will not just happen. Take an initiative, base what you do on sound analysis, and make it make a difference to your job and your career.

Meantime, whatever you do it must be performed effectively if it is to act as a springboard for the future.

step

ENSURING EXCELLENCE: (AND NOT CONFUSING ACTIVITY WITH ACHIEVEMENT)

"You have to have total responsibility for winning. It's never fate. It's always you."

KIRK STEVENS

There is a saying that, in business, one must never confuse activity with achievement. It is true. Never deceive yourself that being busy, applying yourself, putting in the hours or whatever, scores many points. It may not score any. What is noticed is results. When it is said, within a particular organization, that promotion is *on merit* it means, putting it bluntly, that you will only make progress if you succeed in your current role. So things that improve your effectiveness will, in turn, help your career. That is dependent on your expertise in your chosen role. Here we review some common factors that will help everyone not only to do well in any current job, but also to display evidence of career-enhancing characteristics and improve your profile.

RECOGNIZE AND ACCEPT PARETO'S LAW

This principle, named after the famous Italian economist Vilfredo Pareto, is more popularly known as the 80/20 rule. It has various applications in business and here can be related to the fact that only 20 percent of what you do will have a real effect on results. It is the root cause of the fact that some people in business always seem to complete those things that bring them results and recognition, and others never seem to be other than hidden behind a never reducing "pending" tray. This is true of time and effort.

This may sound harsh, after all you are no doubt busy most of the time and everything seems important at the time, but the principle is a strong one. While the figures will not be exactly 80/20, something very close to the ratio will be the case; the rule is true. What is more it can be applied to specific areas of work as well; for example, 20 percent of meeting time produces 80 percent of the decisions (and very probably 20 percent of the areas in this book will be more relevant and useful to you than the rest). Every job includes numbers of essential activities, those that are key to achieving what the job demands, as well as a profusion of minor activities that, though they have to be done, do not contribute in the same way to success.

Recognizing this is itself a significant step to ensuring that the 20 percent is given due consideration and that, in turn, should prompt you to have a very serious look at time management (discussed next), for both can have a direct effect on your effectiveness and therefore on your being seen to achieve objectives.

MANAGE YOUR TIME EFFECTIVELY

In organizations, you will have noticed that some people always seem to manage their time better than others. Like so much else, this does not just happen. And it is without doubt one of *the* key factors governing success in work and in career. If two people have the same skills and, all other things being equal (which they are not, of course, but the point remains), one manages their time better than the other, then the former may well also make better progress. Managing your time effectively not only allows you to be more productive, doing more as well as being able to concentrate on the key tasks (see the above section on Pareto's Law), but also it will most likely be noticed; it labels you as an achiever.

This is perhaps the classic area of good intentions. Everyone says they are going to manage their time well. Some buy expensive time management systems. But if I had the price of a beer for everyone who has said that and not, if they are honest, done anything about it, then I could have retired instead of writing this book! No system will do it for you—time management is about self-management and therefore about self-discipline. This means it is a habit and, as such, while it may take effort to acquire, the whole process does become easier once you have made a commitment and done some groundwork. What are the key disciplines? (Here we touch on only the essentials; but it's a topic worth some separate study.) Consider the following sequence of action:

1. First, you must plan to plan. You need a system, and it can be a loose-leaf diary or notebook rather than a generic system that allows you to note what you have on the go, to prioritize it, and to progress it. Sensibly it will link to a diary. I have yet to meet

anyone who can truly hold all this in their memory, though some claim to do so; realistically therefore some record is always necessary in writing (or on an electronic system, of course).

2. The second rule is to update your plan regularly. How long this takes depends on the job you do. For the majority of people no more than five minutes will be necessary each day. When you do this is a matter of personal preference—first thing in the morning or as you pack up for the day are times favored by many.

3. So far so good and now the next step—you simply have to do what the plan says!

The last, of course, is where it all tends to become somewhat difficult. So many things conspire to stop you following your plan and it is here that the classic timewasters need controlling: too much time in unproductive meetings, too many interruptions, and too much repetitive administration. You can—must—work at all of these, but two things especially need watching which you can control:

1. Putting off what you dislike or find difficult—it is constantly thinking about a task, shuffling papers, but coming to no conclusion or action that wastes so much time.

2. Spending too much time on the things you like, and this often means the things you believe no one else is able to do as well as you. This is often the worse of the two problems.

If you have ever attended a time management course, you will certainly have been encouraged to keep a time log. It is always a sobering exercise; try it for a couple of weeks and you will soon see where time goes. Almost always a log produces surprises: some things take up very much more time than you think. If you know how you work and what happens to your time, you can work at the details that will make you more productive.

In a sense, it really is true to say, *That's all there is to it*. Time management may be a struggle to get organized, but the principles are, for the most part, common sense. Two final points: do not think that because much of your job is unplannable (perhaps because it is reactive, like the manager of a customer service department who must take customer calls and respond at once, but also has longer-term tasks to plan out and fit in) that you cannot manage it. You must plan the non-reactive time, and the less you have of it the more important it is to utilize it effectively. And consider the old maxim that there is never time to do something properly but always has to be time to do something again. Regularly you will find that to sort something may take half an hour or an hour instead of ten minutes. The temptation is to get it done and out of the way, rather than pause and take longer. Take that time once, however, and you may save five minutes every day in future. That may not sound much, but given the average number of working days in the year that could save around 20 hours; maybe every year thereafter.

This is a most important area. Unless you get to grips with it you will be at a serious disadvantage compared with those who do. Become a master of your time and you become able to be more effective, both your results and the way you are seen will improve, and this is one more aid to an advancing career.

NEVER FORGET COMMITMENTS

In my first job, I was hired as what was euphemistically called a "management trainee"; more realistically I was a glorified office boy (I escaped into the sales side of the company). I worked for a boss who was the best kind of mentor and from whom I learned a great deal. Early on, I became convinced he had an infallible memory or used something akin to magic. He *never* seemed to forget anything. He would ask me to do something: "Have a think about it and we will discuss it at the end of the month," he would say. And come the day if I was not at his office door with it at 9:00 a.m., the phone on my desk would ring and he would say, "Now, what about the discussion we planned . . ." He would do this with a couple of dozen people all around the office, registering many, many points with each. In other words, if he told you he would let you have something, or would do something—whatever—he would do it; and on the rare occasions where something prevented it, he would forewarn you of it.

This is a good characteristic to find in a boss and it is a good one to display *to* a boss. Reliability is approved, it is efficient—knowing something will be as planned may be important—and it keeps the majority of contacts you have with more senior managers positive. You do not want their automatic recall of you to be of the endless chasers that they have to make, but that they regard as unnecessary.

My boss owed none of his reputation in this area to magic. He simply had a good system. He had a page in a loose-leaf diary for each person who worked for him, and kept a record of projects large and small linked to his diary. It worked well, and if you build up the reputation of always honoring commitments, whichever way around, that will work well for you.

ALWAYS HIT DEADLINES

Although deadlines are commitments, timing is worth a word in its own right. You do not just need to remember and do *what* the commitment entails but do it by *when* it was arranged. It is said there was never a deadline in history that was not negotiable. This may be true and there is certainly no merit in being pushed somehow into agreeing to a deadline that you cannot possibly meet. It may need negotiation, or at least discussion. Once set, however, a deadline—your deadline—takes on another characteristic, it becomes irrevocable. It can do your reputation nothing but good to be known as someone who delivers on time—not just the major projects and not just when senior people are involved, but everything. Once you have said, "I will make sure you have it next Friday" or something similar, everyone should *know* it will be done.

Always think through any task before agreeing to any particular timing. The more complex the task, the more important this is. Something may appear straightforward, but it is only when you reach stage four perhaps that complications set in and this needs to be built into your estimate of how long it will take—no doubt among the other things you have on your plate. Sometimes in organizations, there is a confusing incidence of what might be called "deadline abuse." That is, someone wants something on, let us say, May 31, so they build in a safety factor and say they need it by May 25. But people know this is what happens, so it is accepted with the thought that the person always builds in a week or so, and that June 2/3 will do. The more people are involved in this scenario the more rapidly it gets much more complicated—and the only thing you can be sure of is that there will be a muddle. Deadlines should be honestly stated and then dealt with accordingly.

Treat deadlines with care and you will help your colleagues and others who are dependent on them being hit, and that in turn will help you.

DECIDE THE RIGHT PRIORITIES

First things first, it is said. Which is a reminder of another area, something that may be viewed as part of time management, the simple matter of setting priorities. Simple may seem the wrong choice of word and, of course, priority setting is not necessarily easy. But it is a simple fact of life that you can only complete one task at a time. First, you do one thing and then you do another, and another. Sometimes you have to pause in one thing to tackle something else. This may be an interruption like a call, but, for the moment, it becomes a priority (otherwise you should offer to call back later!). Busy people often spend a great deal of time in trying to achieve impossibilities. If you can only do one thing at a time (and you can) then you must decide which task takes priority. Of course you may be progressing a number of things at the same time and this must be built into the decision.

Some things need more time spent on them than others. It may be a priority to make a promised call to someone on a particular day. It will take only a few minutes. A different task, like writing this book, may well have a deadline but the work needs to be spread over a large number of days. When things change, and you accept and add a new priority, you need to recalculate. For example, if I promise to deliver the manuscript for this book on a set date and things I could not predict at the time interfere, then there are not so many options; I can:

- Work harder, long into the evening perhaps

- Delay some other task

- Delay the deadline (which may mean getting the agreement of someone else)

The temptation is to struggle on trying to do far too much for a while and then end up with something, or several somethings, done inadequately—or late.

Those with whom you work would no doubt love it if nothing unpredictable happened in your life and you were able to do everything exactly as you wanted. For the most part they do understand that this is simply not real life; changes do occur. Realistically, to return to my example, it may be better for me to say to the publisher a month ahead of the deadline, *I am afraid I will be a week late*, than to struggle on attempting to meet the time and end up not only missing it, but also giving them no notice and perhaps making a mess of some other task along the way. For the record, the manuscript was on time!

There is much talk these days of stress at work and of managing it; books are written about it and courses conducted on it. But stress is, it seems to me, a reaction to circumstances rather than what the circumstances themselves do to you. Clear job definition and clear objectives, mentioned earlier, should make it easier to decide priorities. Certainly a realistic attitude to how you arrange your work and what gets done first, second, and third makes for greater effectiveness. Nothing is achieved just by panicking or sitting around and wondering what to do or wishing the priority decision did not have to be made. Concern and constructive thought about how to sort something are positive. Worry is negative. What do all these thoughts have to do with your career?

Rapid and clear decisions made about your priorities—a continual process for most busy executives (often noted in time management systems)—will make you more effective. Clarity of thought and decisiveness are both qualities looked for in more senior management. Learning to be philosophical about the things that cause stress and concentrating your thinking on the practicalities of what will work best will reduce worry and get more done. And the whole thrust of this section is to show how increased effectiveness, and the impression that it gives, improves your career prospects.

ALWAYS ON TARGET

In many organizations the culture is, in one respect, very straightforward. People who hit targets are regarded as achieving something and doing what is required. This is most obvious where there are numbers involved. If productivity was targeted to go up 10 percent but goes up 11 percent instead, then this is good. And it is always clearest of all when the target is financial. It is, after all, money that keeps the organizational wheels turning. As an example, someone on the sales side consistently hitting their sales target is much more likely to be promoted than a colleague whose results are down, and consistently missing targets in such an area is often the best route to early "retirement." This is a powerful career influencer, and if you doubt just how powerful it is then, again, on the sales side you can note that it is quite often seen that the best salesperson in an organization is promoted (even though they sometimes make a poor sales manager—after all the qualities and tasks the two jobs require are very different).

The career implications of this are very clear. Because you are significantly more likely to register as doing a good job if you are consistently hitting your target (much more so than in a, perhaps apparently appealing, *laissez-faire* situation) you may want to consider:

- Suggesting that your job should include some targets if it does not—especially, if possible, financial ones—or indeed putting some numbers to it and suggesting the actual targets

- Making sure any such targets are realistic; especially targets that someone else does set for you. Some review, indeed some negotiation, here may be advisable

- Making sure any such agreed targets are regularly reviewed, and also reported, although crowing about them too loudly if they are hit may be self-defeating

Some would even say that jobs where measurement of success is inherently difficult are to be avoided, though such a job may offer other advantages. Generally speaking, though, a target hit or exceeded is always useful to the careerist. It is also motivational—most of us like to know all is going well rather than just believing it is.

DO MORE THAN IS EXPECTED OF YOU

This seems an obviously good thing, and certainly there are derogatory remarks that conjure up the opposite; we talk, for instance, of people *scraping through*, just doing sufficient to get by. This latter is not the attitude upon which careers thrive. So, delivering more than others expect is, not surprisingly, to be recommended.

This does not mean, however, that work has to take over your life and that "more" is produced as a result of excessive hours worked. It seems to be a fact that all the jobs that are themselves interesting or worth while do demand more than the regular "9 to 5" attitude (certainly this is my experience; if you have found something that is interesting, pays well, and makes few demands, please let me know!). So, accepting that, you need to be sufficiently industrious to create the right results and the right image. Remember, there are two sides to every coin. Being consistently in the office for overlong hours could imply a sign of inefficiency and that you are unable to cope.

Probably the most important way to deliver more is to think more about things than is necessary to do the job. For example, imagine you are asked to write a report on how your department's efficiency might be improved. This could be entirely introspective and based in the present, and you can come up with some perfectly good ideas for reducing costs or whenever the brief might be. Or you could take a broader view, maybe improvements are only possible by two departments working more closely together, or maybe there are advantages to be taken that link in, and are only made possible by events that you know are coming in future. I am not suggesting that the specifics of this example apply everywhere, but the process of thinking involved is clear and may well produce more.

The same principle applies to seemingly much smaller issues. I sit on a small committee, and the Chair always produces and circulates in advance a detailed agenda. It is not strictly necessary in terms of the complexity of the issues, but it is useful to those present—the Chair does just a little more than is strictly necessary, and it shows. Be known as one who operates this way and it will be one more thing that can help you to be seen in the right light.

BE OPEN-MINDED

Nothing will stultify effectiveness and progress inside an organization more than a closed mind. There is a saying that you can have either, say, five years' experience, or the same year's experience repeated five times. A closed mind goes through the same processes and thus the same experience. It is now routine to say that we live in dynamic times and that the pace of change is increasing, but that does not mean it is not true. The open-minded will cope better with changes. You will have to accept, get to grips with, and use new approaches, ideas, and technologies in the future. You may already see some of these looming and others may be difficult if not impossible to imagine or predict today, but they will come nevertheless.

For many, the best example of the moment continues to be information technology (IT) with computers as a major element of it. The current generation are growing up with it and, to some extent, take it in their stride. Others ignore it completely, and others still struggle to make sense of it all. I have already referred to my writing as an example, but learning to type and use word processing software did require a major shift in attitude at the time.

Most people must constantly take on board new ideas if their career is to progress. Sometimes these will be major areas, as above; at other times it is a question of minor, but significant points—finding a way to work with a new, and seemingly difficult, colleague perhaps. Whatever the job you do there will be such changes to cope with. You must guard against getting so set in your ways that you do not respond positively to these developments large and small, and like so much else you must be seen to be open-minded. It will secure your effectiveness over both the short and long term and make a contribution to the way your career progresses.

BE HONEST

Honesty is the best policy and, in business as in life, this is usually the case. I suppose I must say usually here, because it is sadly true to say there are some people in some organizations who rise up the ranks and do well on out and out deception. It happens. And many of us have probably come across people who fall into this category; though we can take comfort from the fact that the longer they pursue this line, the more vulnerable they become to discovery. Not only that, but there are areas where large numbers of people are regularly dishonest. For instance, research (in Britain) has shown that some 20 percent of people applying for new jobs complete the necessary application forms dishonestly, and this does not just include minor embellishments. They will claim to have degrees from universities that they have never attended, and twice I have heard of people being taken on to do jobs where they received and needed to use a company car and then it was discovered that their claim to be able to drive was a lie!

So the truth of the matter is that while you may prosper by lying, you only have to get found out once and any good it may have done in the past is lost forever. In any case most people do want to achieve whatever they do on their own merits; there can surely be no real and lasting satisfaction in conning your way through.

Honesty is the best policy, not least people around you should know that you are honest and keep your word; additionally, honesty links to trust, which is an important factor in getting on in any organization.

One additional point: always start as you mean to go on. For instance, when you move into a new position you must aim to make a positive impact fast, in both what you achieve and how you are seen. Another book in this series can help here: *New Kid on the Block* by Frances Kay.

For many readers a key aspect of being effective in their jobs involves how they manage others, and this is addressed in this last section of this chapter. So, if you are a manager now this is relevant; so is it too if you see this as part of your career path.

MANAGING PEOPLE

Many people who work in an organization find that progress involves an increasing responsibility for managing other people. This is natural enough given the structure of most organizations. In some jobs, based on a specialist expertise, progress seems to involve a situation where the work involved consists less and less of the specialist expertise and more and more of management and administration. It is, however, easier to develop administrative skills than to develop management ones. The points in this section are not intended to be any kind of comprehensive review of how to be a manager (this is a wide topic and one that you may want to review separately); rather, they are designed to highlight those factors that have a direct bearing on your ability to do the job and progress your career.

MANAGE WELL

People management is a complex set of skills and processes and is another of those things in business life where excellence does not just happen. Good managers may make it look easy; but this is deceptive. They need to work at it, and only by having a clear view of what is necessary and being prepared to give the whole process the time and consideration it demands, can they make it appear to happen without problem. So the first rule is to take any involvement that you may have in management very seriously.

Some people see management as an end in itself. They obtain challenge and satisfaction from managing a team of people and producing results from their efforts. (A good definition of management is that it is *achieving results through other people*. It is thus very different from what you actually do yourself.) Others find the whole process a distraction from whatever they see as the real job in hand. If you are in the latter category, then make no mistake, it is not something you can ignore; if management is a necessary part of the job you do, or even a job you do en route to something else, then you have to do it and do it well. Nothing will show you up in a worse light than being in charge of a group of people who become unhappy and demotivated because they are poorly managed, and who perform poorly as a result.

Overall the management process must successfully influence your people to ensure they implement an agreed plan and do so effectively. It has to blend setting up the tasks involved, and doing so in a way that works with the individuals and also respects the entity of the team involved. Your skills in achieving the required results through the group must be matched by your skill in managing the relationships of individuals within the team.

The essentials of the management process, which should focus on the tasks and the team, are:

- **Defining objectives:** identifying tasks and restraints and setting targets

- **Planning:** and deciding priorities

- **Communicating:** to brief, instruct, and check understanding

- **Supporting and controling:** monitoring progress, checking, and adapting

- **Evaluating:** reviewing whether and how results have been achieved

- **Linking to the future:** ensuring experience helps make things better in future

Make excellence in management your goal: assemble the right team, develop and motivate them, and their performance will reflect well on every aspect of your career. The further points in this section look at individual aspects of the process that are important in this way.

WORK WITH YOUR PEOPLE, NOT AGAINST THEM

Of course, managers must manage. It does not just happen and results are important. But some managers seem to have or develop a very confrontational style (I know, I once worked for one), and this is, in my view, much less likely to produce results and is certainly less motivational for all concerned.

You will achieve most by ensuring that your team perform effectively. If you treat people as competition, if you restrict rather than encourage what they do, there is a good chance they will perform less well, and their results reflect on you—whatever they are. You must work *with* a team, through a team, and you need their support. Think of managers whom you have worked for in the past, or at present. Ask yourself:

- What characteristics do they have that you like?

- Are you learning something in working for them?

- Do they delegate rather than keep everything to themselves?

- Do they take the credit rather than give it?

- Are they fair?

- Are they inappropriately secretive?

You can probably think of many more criteria. Whatever you put on such a list, consider your people. What do they want from you as a manager? None of this means you cannot be firm where necessary, run a tight ship, and not suffer fools gladly. Management may well need such attitudes as well, but the whole effect must come over at the end of the day in a way that carries people with you. You must not let people try to run before they can walk, but with things properly set up, if you give them their head people may well give you a great deal more.

HELP PEOPLE DEVELOP

This is important; no one wants to do the same job repetitively forever and ever. Market and environment factors in any case make most jobs dynamic; keeping up with the changes is part of what must happen, so jobs should not become static. But people respond to a challenge, they want to learn, to do new things and old things better and you must not see this as a threat. There is a real fear in some managers that allowing people to develop risks them taking the credit if not taking over. Two points need considering here:

1. First, managing a team means just that—the manager cannot do everything; indeed, the effectiveness of the section is dependent on the productivity of the whole team. If you do not delegate, or develop others to do more and more, little progress will be possible. If you do, then some of the work moves out of your hands but the effectiveness of the whole effort will increase, and the potential of a team that performs well far outstrips that of any one individual.

2. Secondly, there is a valuable maxim to the effect that you cannot have the authority and the credit. This means that trying to organize so that everything reflects well on you achieves less than giving the credit to others as what they do expands. You

take your own credit in terms of respect for a well-managed team producing results.

Developing others, with all that that entails, will develop your results and your recognition.

MOTIVATE PEOPLE

Motivation is a complex set of principles and processes within the overall management task. Put simply, people perform best when they enjoy what they do and feel it is appreciated. This is, like so much else, not something that happens of its own volition. It takes time, and it is time that some managers begrudge, feeling that time is better spent *actually doing something* rather than helping people along who should be able to look after themselves.

But we cannot change human nature. People need motivation (don't you?), and the time spent on what is a continual process is well worth while in terms of the difference it makes to results. This is a well-researched area. What must be done and how is too big a topic to go into in the space available here. Suffice it to say that motivation must *minimize* those aspects of work that tend to worry people (called dissatisfiers, and concerned primarily with environmental factors such as policy, administration, and work conditions) and *maximize* the impact of those things that create good feelings (the motivators, which are mainly job related with the most important usually being regarded as achievement and recognition).

Some of these demand action with people on an individual basis, some with the team. Action ranges from the simplest form of motivation: just saying "Thank you" or "Well done" (and how many of us can really put our hand on our heart and say we do this sufficiently often?), to complex reward schemes, incentives, and other more tangible tactics.

Managing in an environment of low motivation is twice as hard as when things are going well in this respect. Attitude and thus, in turn, performance are directly affected by the motivational "climate." Do not neglect this area; a good team is an asset to the career of anyone with management responsibilities.

KEEP IN TOUCH

Successful management cannot be conducted from behind a closed office door. If you are to have a well-motivated team, if you are to achieve results, create and maintain satisfactory quality standards— whatever you have to do, you have to be in touch with the people. Way back, it was the American book *In Search of Excellence* that coined the phrase *management by walking about* (M.B.W.A.). This means exactly what it says, coupled with the recommendation that you do not just see them, you *talk* to them.

This happens in two ways.

1. First, you have to be accessible. People need to be able to come to you when necessary (not to waste time feeling they should be able to cope). Not least they should feel free, indeed be encouraged, to make suggestions, feed in ideas, and contribute in whatever ways make sense to the smooth running of the operation in which they are involved.

2. Secondly, you have to go to them, something that takes more effort if they are not nearby, for the principle is the same whether the people concerned are in the next door office, in the field like salespeople or engineers, or in another office or location—which may be an office a short drive away or your operation's overseas outpost. You have to see what they are up to, be seen to do so, check how things are going, understand the situation on their ground, and be sufficiently informed as a result to make the decisions you need to do, and do so wisely. Again this will not only contribute to the results you make happen, it is the right way to be seen and has added career benefits in the sense that you really know what is going on across a broad front.

There is a saying that you do not have to be able to lay eggs to be a chicken farmer! Similarly, you do not have to be able to do all the tasks those on your team have to undertake, but it surely helps if you understand something about them, and the people doing them, and if this knowledge is up to date. So resolve to be the manager who walks about, and does so regularly and with purpose.

ADOPT THE RIGHT MANAGEMENT STYLE

No one manages in exactly the same way, nor is there some textbook form of doing so that should be followed slavishly. Quite apart from anything else, you cannot make yourself work in a way that is simply contrary to your normal instincts and manner. Style could be taken as encompassing everything that is done in managing, but here I want to concentrate on only three points, not least because I feel they are important if you are to become an effective manager and to develop a style of management that is likely to be approved and thus benefit your career.

1. **Be fair:** There are few things that people dislike more in a manager than unfairness. This is not, however, the same as being democratic (few organizations are, nor is it usually any recipe for decisive or appropriate action). But to treat people on a similar basis, not play favorites, and be seen only to make decisions for the benefit of the general good has to be right.

2. **Be consistent:** To a degree, this goes with being fair and a first comment is necessarily similar: people hate working for someone who runs hot and cold, who is all sweetness and light one minute and fire and brimstone the next. So a consistent approach gets the best from people, but this relates somewhat obviously to promotion decisions—would you select someone for a job if they were very inconsistent in this way or would you see it as taking a disproportionate risk? The latter seems more likely.

3. **Be consultative:** All the best advice about management style seems to indicate that the days of a dictatorial approach, one that simply tells people what to do, have long gone. People expect to be consulted to some extent (though my point about democracy above stands). Not only that, but only through consultation and discussion can you orchestrate the full power of

your people in terms of ideas and effectiveness. It takes more time, but in the long run if more goes well as a result this will save time.

What you do here needs some conscious thought and considered action. In career terms too you can do worse than observe and analyze what seems to be the preferred style of management by looking at the kinds of people who are moving successfully up the hierarchy. These may well share certain approaches; indeed, there is a phenomenon called mirror recruitment through which management only select people who exhibit all their own characteristics, good or bad! While you should not copy an organizational style slavishly it may well be worth accommodating certain clearly preferred characteristics.

Being a good manager gives you an additional and significant platform from which to work your career plan. While individual members of a team can cause transient problems, managed the right way, your staff will always have a positive effect on your career.

Much of what has been said in this chapter and earlier too may sound as if it can be applied easily, that being effective is straightforward and unencumbered by any restraints. Not so, of course. You have to make these things happen. What is more, the workplace can be a complex, and sometimes hostile, environment. And sometimes, as we see in the next chapter, it gets political.

Do everything necessary to achieve the results you are charged with; more than that aim to deliver an excellent performance that will enhance your "career profile."

OFFICE POLITICS: SURVIVING IN A VOLATILE ENVIRONMENT

66 Politics is the art of looking for trouble, finding it whether it exists or not, diagnosing it incorrectly, and applying the wrong remedy. **99**

SIR ERNEST BENN

The office where office politics do not exist does not exist. There are political office environments, very political ones—and not much else. Taking a stance and action in light of this is a much more difficult area than some in which to plan consciously to excel. Political factors contain aspects that can exert dramatic influences— such as a company unexpectedly bought out by new owners who see change, including replacing people, as the way ahead—and over which you may have little control. Nor should political tactics be seen as a magic formula for success as the ruthless politician contrives his or her way to the top through an unstoppable series of coups (though this does happen).

On the other hand, there are some principles here that can be treated in just the same way as the other plans you make and tasks you set yourself with an eye on advancement.

MATCH YOURSELF TO THE CORPORATE CULTURE

I mean this in a practical and considered sense, and in two rather different ways that are perhaps best described by an example. First, before I set up my own business, I worked in a medium-sized consultancy firm employing about one hundred people. What made the firm profitable was having sufficient work of the right kind, at the right time, and the right fee level. The culture of the firm reflected this fact. Two key ways in which people were judged were:

1. Self-sufficiency—producing a volume of work they could do profitably and hitting their own financial targets.

2. Selling more work than they could do personally and thus helping fill the work schedules of others less skillful at selling.

Of course, there were other things, not least quality of work. But, though it would sometimes be denied, the two above were most important and someone doing excellent work but not hitting their target, maybe by a small margin, would not be so well regarded.

Without a doubt, being self-sufficient and selling more than you could do helped someone get on within the firm. Every organization has such factors as these and you would do well to think on what they are and what action you should take to get the most from the situation.

Secondly, though perhaps less practically linked to organizational work, there are other more social factors. An organization may build up a core of senior people who share the same interests or activities. In one firm, this may mean many internal decisions are made on the golf course, or in a particular bar after office hours. This may be more difficult to fit in with, and just taking up golf or whatever may not see you instantly welcomed into the inner sanctum anyway, but should be observed and considered.

This is less a question of being what might be called a "company person" than of taking the most practical opportunities offered (the consultancy example above is a good one in this respect); apart from anything else you do not want to be seen to be striving to "fit in" in a contrived way as this is self-defeating in terms of the effect it will have on others.

ASSESS AND KNOW THE OPPOSITION

Teamwork is essential to any successful enterprise. Yet it is simply not true to imagine that an organization is simply one big, happy family with everyone sharing the same feelings and ambitions. All organizations are to one degree or another hierarchical and all are pyramid shaped. There are, as they say, more Indians than Chiefs. Inevitably, therefore, people within an organization are in competition with each other, not equally for everything, of course, but how you progress will be influenced, in part at least, by how others, particularly those with similar intentions, progress.

Your own career plans should therefore reflect an active and ongoing appraisal of this fact. Consider: who specially is likely to influence your progress in the particular direction you have set your sights on? And how are they likely to proceed with their career plan? Honest and open (though there are always unseen undercurrents) competition is to be expected. However, out and out politicking is much less to be recommended, though of course it does happen, and if the knives are out then self-defense has to be the order of the day. Unfortunately, this kind of approach tends to be bad for the organization, breeding suspicion, lowering motivation, and resulting in more time being spent watching backs than on the job in hand. Additionally it can create confusion, which similarly distracts from the real tasks and issues.

However such things proceed, you should take how it works, and in particular other people, into your thinking and act in a way that assesses realistically how it all changes the situation. Sometimes such an assessment will send you off on another tack, or into another organization, for there are those where the cut and thrust is simply too much for some. On other occasions you have to resolve and gear up for fierce competition. But perhaps achieving success would be no fun if it were too easy!

WATCH FOR SIGNS OF LIKELY CHANGE

Horror stories abound of signs of impending doom. In one American company it was said that the signs of your personal position faltering involved the telephone. Occasionally someone would sit down at their desk and find their phone was "dead." On contacting the operator to report the fact (using another phone), a polite voice would inform them that they no longer needed a telephone. Unpleasant. Here I mean to commend the simple, practical advice of keeping an ear to the ground and your wits about you.

Sometimes someone says that they are *too busy for politics* just before something occurs to their disadvantage; something that they would have seen coming a mile away if they had only looked up. Being busy, for whatever reason—and I have commended being productive as a means to success elsewhere—must not blind you to what is going on around you. I once saw some office graffiti saying

It is difficult to see the writing on the wall if your back's to it. It is a fair point.

Of course, we must remain constructive. The reason to watch for signs is only in part to watch for warning signs; it is also to watch for opportunities. For example, in one company two executives worked closely together and got on well. One day the more senior of the two confided that he was seeking to work overseas. "In a year or so I will be on the other side of the world," he said. On the day he duly resigned, his colleague was able to put a report on the joint boss's desk recommending he took over as the department head, showing why he was well equipped to do so and how he could rapidly re-staff to fill the gap he would leave. What is more, he had made sure during that year, when he knew what was likely to occur, that he took some self-development action to make sure he had a good chance of the plan being approved. Is that office politics or sensibly taking advantage of circumstances?

NEVER CUT OFF YOUR OPTIONS

I think this heading states the most sensible and useful piece of advice I have ever been given in this area. Realistically the options you have, indeed the options you build into your career plan, are more like a river constantly branching into tributaries than one straight road. There is rarely advantage in rejecting privately, or taking action that rules out, any particular path. Unless you are genuinely clairvoyant (in which case what are you doing reading this? You *know* what level of success you will achieve!), you never know which will be the best route. Circumstances change. What seemed like a long shot suddenly becomes a real possibility, or what seemed secondary becomes your best option—provided you have not ruled it out. So keep all your options open and only do away with any for good reason (it is possible sacrificing one will open up another, and perhaps a better one, but this should be a conscious decision).

Career planning has a good deal in common with strategy. You need to take a strategic view and the rule discussed here is in fact just one aspect of this process. At the risk of introducing yet another topic you need to know about, you could do worse than to read a little about strategy and, if you want to give business books a rest for a moment, read James Clavell's book about Japan: *Shōgun*; it has more in it about strategy than most titles with the word in the title (and it is an enthralling read).

SYMBOLS OF SUCCESS

Somebody once coined the term "executive toys" for desk gadgetry of various sorts; primarily for the tacky type such as those things that roll stainless steel balls into holes marked *yes* and *no* to aid decision-making. The choice of such things, if any, should be treated with care.

Some people go to some pains to cultivate an image in this way, ensuring that they have the right newspapers or magazines around the office, that the clock shows three different time zones, and the wall and bookshelves are stocked with the right kind of pictures, certificates, and business titles to show that the office is occupied by a thrusting and high powered executive.

The trouble is that many of these things can backfire. The clock may not be seen as a symbol of international connections but as pretentious. Someone who has actually read one of the books might ask you about its content and so on. Probably the only reasonable advice is moderation and care. Personally I would settle for surroundings that are straightforward and businesslike rather than risk something being taken the wrong way. That is not to say that you cannot have a few homely touches, though it is good if even they have some relevance. Among other things on my office wall is a print showing an original illustration from Lewis Carroll's famous book *Alice in Wonderland*. The words reproduced alongside the picture of Alice in conversation with the Cheshire Cat run as follows:

"Would you tell me, please, which way I ought to go from here?"

"That depends a good deal on where you want to get to," said the Cat.

"I don't very much care where . . ." said Alice.

"Then it doesn't matter which way you go," said the Cat.

"... so long as I get somewhere," Alice added as an explanation.

"Oh, you're sure to do that," said the Cat, "if only you walk long enough."

As a plea for clear objectives this is not a bad motto for a business; or for a career. Anyway, *I like* it.

BE A LITTLE PARANOID

Assessing the opposition was touched on earlier, but took a reasonable view of opposition as those who are, for whatever reason, in competition with you, directly or indirectly. Sometimes, however, and it pays to be realistic about this, opposition has an altogether more sinister meaning to it. Remember the saying *Just because you are paranoid doesn't mean people aren't out to get you*—many a true word is spoken in jest and organizations can sometimes have something about them of the law of the jungle. Some people, only a few one hopes, are destructive for no good reason, or are spiteful or, for whatever reason, are just not on your side and happy to see you fall by the wayside.

I do not wish to give the impression that this is a major factor (much less encourage unpleasant in-fighting), but this book would be incomplete if it omitted any reference to the possibility. Advice? You should be, in a word, watchful. Read between the lines, take a little while to form views of people, be especially wary in difficult or changing times—adversity sometimes brings out the worst in people—and treat remarks like "Trust me" with a degree of caution. There may not be an assassin hiding around every corner, but you may well meet one or two over the longer term. Forewarned is forearmed.

It is possible to be too cynical about office politics. It is a thorny area. As the economist J. K. Galbraith said: *Politics is not the art of the possible. It consists of choosing between the disastrous and the unpalatable.* It is also possible (easy?) to fail to consider it enough. Be warned.

Overall, what is required here is an awareness of the political nature of the workplace and a resolve to accommodate what this implies into your career planning.

step **9**

YOUR PROFILE:
LOOKING SUCCESSFUL

"Only fools do not judge by appearances.

OSCAR WILDE

It is sometimes said, for example of advertising, that *perception is reality*. In other words, people will usually base their judgment on what they see of something; so too with people. Think of someone in your organization perhaps whom you do not know very much about. Ask yourself what you think about them: are they busy? Competent? Approachable? Expert? Ambitious? Efficient? If they are a manager, what do you think their staff think of them? You will find that if you make yourself draw conclusions from any evidence, many questions can apparently be asked and answered and a reasonable picture builds up. You feel that you can judge something about them. Whether it is true or not is, of course, another matter. Our very visibility gives out many signals, and will do so whether we think about it consciously or not. Here we review some of the ways in which you can give signals that paint the right kind of picture of you in a career-enhancing way that will create an image compatible with your career intentions.

LOOK THE PART

I once attended an evening talk of a professional institute and heard someone give a review of what are sometimes called "beauty parades" or competitive presentations. He made a number of interesting points including the simple advice: look the part. He gave a number of detailed examples, one of which was the advice to wear what he called "big-boy shoes" (ones with shoelaces rather than slip-on style). Now this is going a bit far perhaps, but the point is well made—first impressions are largely visual and they are important. So too is someone's prevailing style, how colleagues and others see you around the office and work environment.

Now this is a difficult area to advise on precisely. I am not promoting designer fashion or any specific style of dress, and you have to be reasonably natural, but you want to be seen to take business seriously. You can be smart without spending a fortune, you must always be clean and tidy, and the details matter. The Americans talk about "power dressing." This is a concept that is too contrived for many; indeed, there is a real likelihood that going too far in this way becomes self-defeating, and is just seen as pretentious. It may be important in some jobs to meet the standards and style of those with whom the organization does business rather than internally. Once having met with a major bank to discuss possible training work, a colleague of mine, one who took pride in his appearance, was dismayed that a letter came back requesting the work to be done by someone *shorter in the hair and longer in the tooth!* An older and more traditional alternative was found and the work went well; that is the client's right.

So, what specifically is certain? The following are often mentioned:

- Clean fingernails and tidy hair

- Smart (rather than over-fashionable) clothes

- Clean shoes

And, though it is more difficult to judge, an appropriate spend: I once had an inquiry from someone who said: "One of your competitors has just been to see me and arrived in a Porsche; I think I would like another quote."

Finally, styles and norms differ internationally. A suit is normal business dress in Britain, though a jacket and trousers (not a matching suit) is becoming seen as just as acceptable and some organizations are now much less formal. Shirts and ties are more important in countries where the hot weather precludes jackets—and practice differs in different kinds of business—generally a bank, say, being more formal than an advertising agency. Similarly, men and women have different styles to consider, with the greater choice facing the women frankly making their decisions more difficult.

Whatever your style, whatever you opt for, think about it, relate what you do to the corporate culture and practice and remember your appearance says very much more about you than you might think. You will have an image; the only question is what image will you make it.

CREATE EXTERNAL VISIBILITY

Doing a radio interview, I remember meeting another interviewee who was there to comment on some technical matter. We got chatting and I asked him who he was. He said that he worked for a large company and had made a point of becoming known as the company's expert on the particular technical issue in question. "Do you run the technical department?" I asked him. "No," he said. "But I aim to." Hearing what he did to establish himself as the technical "guru," I was inclined to believe him.

This tale makes a good point—public relations is not only a valuable tool to promote the company, it has career development potential as well. It is tightly linked with some of the communications skills reviewed earlier. My fellow interviewee at the radio studio would not have been there unless he could talk fluently about his chosen topic, just being knowledgable about it was not enough. What is more, if he performed well then he stood a good chance of being asked back.

Radio is perhaps a dramatic example to take, though by no means unattainable, but public relations activity incorporates many different possibilities. Given that you have or can create some expertise worthy of comment, and very many jobs have this possibility, start internally as you review the possibilities, for instance:

- Is there a company magazine or newsletter?

- Are there groups or committees you can take part in or speak at?

- Should you be seeking to write articles?

- Can you speak at the local management institute or trade or professional body?

There may be many options, and this is very much an activity that creates its own momentum. For example, an article published in the company newsletter might be adapted to go in an external publication, a copy of that being sent to a professional body might prompt an invitation to speak and at that meeting you might meet someone who . . . but you get the point.

If such activity grows up naturally, and has a use for the organization as well as for you, then it should not create ripples (though others may well wish they had thought of it first) and it can become an ongoing part of what you do to say to those about you that you are going places. Nothing succeeds like success, they say, and being seen to have achieved these things is certainly potentially useful. See you in the studio.

TAKE AN INTEREST IN YOUR INTERESTS

In many companies, particularly large ones, there is considerable social interaction among staff. Just how much there is and how it works will vary, and is affected by such things as whether there is a social club and where the office is located; some city center locations where people typically travel long distances to work may mean they live as much as a hundred miles apart and this will reduce social possibilities. There will also be a culture within the organization relating to this kind of activity. In some companies, senior people are involved in some of this and others are clearly expected to be. In others, it is seen as a lower level activity and you may not want to get too involved in case you are seen as essentially frivolous.

Another issue here is that, rightly or wrongly, executives have a total image. Though interference in employees' private lives is not the style of many organizations, and would be resented by many staff, you may be expected to have certain interests. Some of these are perfectly reasonable; it is useful for executives, especially those who have contacts outside the firm, to be generally well-informed in terms of current affairs, for example. If you are in a technical area, you may need to keep up to date on a broad range of scientific matters simply to be able to relate well to others you work with. On the other hand, there are organizations where the style of the Chief Executive—evidenced by a passion for, say, golf, science fiction, or undersea diving—is mirrored by aspiring staff around the office forever plunging into the sea or Arthur C. Clarke. Whether this last is useful or not is uncertain. I would like to think it is not, but there are organizations where this kind of fitting in is important. It is certainly worth a thought. You are unlikely to have to rearrange your whole life around such things, but some accommodation with such perception may be useful.

SEX

No, this section will not provide a guide to your love life. It is here for two reasons. First, because the conventional wisdom of publishing is that any book with sex in the contents list will sell more than one without! And, more seriously, because the gender of any individual inevitably has an effect on how they are seen. This is no place for a major debate on women in business; suffice it to say that they are still, in many cultures, not taken as seriously as men. Leaving the reasons on one side, what is the effect? Let me start with an illustration. I used to have a young lady working with me who moved from a secretarial position to one of more executive responsibility and then to a position where she joined a small management committee. Halfway through the first meeting she attended, someone delivered a tray of tea and coffee and left it on a side table. Discussion continued and, after a few minutes, she got up, poured, and handed around the drinks.

After the meeting, she asked me how she had got on. She had done well, contributing some sound comments, but I remember saying, "Why did you pour the tea?" She did not hesitate, saying at once, "Right, I won't do that again." Now I am not suggesting that every woman early in a management career is in danger of being typecast as the tea lady, or secretary/hostess, and it did not in fact matter who did the chore; the point is that perceptions stick. Sometimes women are in danger of being underrated and thus, rightly or wrongly, they have to think twice as hard as a man about how they are seen. So, in my view, she was right to decide not to engage with the tea tray again (and her subsequent progress proved she was ultimately very much seen in the right light). Of course, women can increasingly fight their corner, and I like the quotation attributed to Charlotte Whitten: *Whatever women do, they must do twice as well as men to be thought half as good. Luckily, this is not difficult.* Even so, this area may need some conscious thought.

Similarly, and for everyone, there is merit in making sure all dealings around the organization are on the basis of jobs done, expertise, and merit rather than gender (whichever is involved). However, in organizations the world over people will continue to say: "How about dinner?" Regarding this as anything to do with career development runs the risk of getting you into very deep water.

DO NOT DRINK IN EXCESS

This is common sense, but worth a word. In many businesses, a certain amount of socialising is not only pleasant, but it is also part of the way the business works. On the other hand, someone being the worse for drink helps few, if any, decisions and most, if not all, management will prefer to promote the office cat before promoting someone with even a suspicion of a drinking problem. Enough said.

GIVE AND TAKE

It would be difficult and, given the many different types of job and styles of organization in the world, not even helpful to set out a perfect package of characteristics for those wanting to develop their careers. One point is, however, worth a thought. It may seem that a dedication to developing a career demands a selfish outlook, and to some degree this may be true. But think also of the effect a selfish attitude in others has on you. It is not the most endearing characteristic imaginable.

Success and effectiveness is assisted by cooperation. Teamwork has been mentioned elsewhere, and a selfish attitude to others hardly encourages their cooperation in ways that will help you or your organizational objectives.

When I first went into consulting, I worked with a group of people who were less selfish than any other I have encountered before or since. No one ever seemed too busy to help. You could walk into any office and get advice, information, and support of all kinds— from just a word to a complete rundown on something (and if it could not be given at once a time was set). Information was regarded as for sharing, not for exclusive hoarding, and the whole firm, far from grinding to a halt because time was taken in this way, seemed to thrive on the attitude. For a newcomer, it was a godsend and I made full use of the learning and accelerated experience it provided and, in due course, found myself part of the network spending time giving as well as receiving.

There is an altruistic side to this attitude. You never know in an organization how things will go and how things will turn out. The person whose head you bite off because they want a moment of your time when you are busy, turns up next a year later in a position of authority or influence and with not the slightest intention of sharing anything with you. You cannot have too many allies. A point was made in Step 8 about assessing and dealing with the opposition. The reverse applies also and this is one way that, while benefiting the company, cultivates more allies than enemies.

AVOID BEING TYPECAST

Every kind of business activity seems to run this risk. In my own business, it is very difficult to stop some clients seeing me exclusively as a consultant, others seeing me exclusively as a trainer or a writer (though I work at it!). Some companies have a similar problem in selling the range of what they make; they are known for one or two main items and the others always seem to get left behind. There can be a similar situation with people as a career progresses, and sometimes the effect can be negative.

For example, the Greeks used to execute messengers bringing bad news. It cannot have made the bad news go away but it must, I suppose, have made them all feel better; well, not the messengers! In any company, people can take on a series of tasks. Some tasks play to their strengths, they are important and have to be done; but there are also some tasks that tend to create a negative image of the individual. If you become known as the person who closed down the troublesome plant, subsequently made 300 people redundant, axed the firm's oldest and dearest product, and canceled the research everyone felt would herald a new era of successful innovation, then you probably won't be the most popular person in the company.

Now there is considerable danger in making decisions just to be popular, and I am not suggesting either that hard decisions should not be faced or that they should be fudged. Equally, there are professional troubleshooters who do nothing but this sort of thing and manage to retain a positive profile in the organization for which they work. But one still might conclude that there are certain activities and tasks that are better avoided if your subsequent profile and career are not to be blighted. Even if the blight is small you may be better off without it. It is difficult to offer more specific advice but the point is worth keeping in mind, and should you feel exposed in this kind of way at least you can take action to rebalance the effect.

Be aware: every aspect of how you appear plays a role in how you are seen. As the examples here have shown, the range of things is considerable (and there are others from the state of your desk to your manner when conducting a meeting); so it is worth some thought and some care to get it right. How you appear should be largely the result of deciding how you *want* to appear. If you make good judgments about that, it will stand you in good stead.

To end on a slightly philosophical note, I will quote Jean-Paul Sartre who said: *Things are entirely what they appear to be and behind them . . . there is nothing*. This emphasizes that this is not an area you can afford to ignore.

 Know the kind of profile you want to have, in detail, and work at everything that helps to create, maintain, and project it.

step **10**

MOVING ON:

ONWARD AND UPWARD

"If you want to do something, you find a way. If you don't want to do anything, you find an excuse."

ARAB PROVERB

Few people spend their entire career with one employer; indeed, the average number of jobs in a career is increasing. Furthermore, some of those few who do stay longer are in large multinational entities, which are a conglomeration of different companies. So you may well come to the point where changing jobs and organizations is the only way you see the possibility of continuing to develop your career. This book, as you know, is not presenting a blueprint for finding a new job, but there are some issues here that fit our brief and that you should have in mind well before taking steps to do so.

CHOOSE THE RIGHT MOMENT TO GO

Get the timing wrong and the funniest story will fall flat. Get the timing wrong in a career and the same can happen. You need to consider this from two angles: first, when you should initiate action to seek another appointment, and secondly, when it is right to take advantage of an opportunity that presents itself.

In both cases, the thinking starts with a review of the prospects within your existing situation. If you have a plan (and if you did not before, then by this stage of reading through this book you should have), that is the place to start. Is it likely that a new position would better enable you to reach your objectives than continued progress where you are now? You have to balance the "devil you know" against something inherently less known, but, quite possibly, no more difficult to predict. For many people the temptation to stay put and not, as they see it, take a risk is very great. On the other hand, if the offer comes to you, that always feels flattering and may be difficult to resist as you compare a current employer, where your progress is slower than you would wish, with someone who is offering an immediate change and rise in salary.

Several issues may form a part of the decision as to whether to move:

- **Predictability:** In some organizations formal career planning is well spelled out. You know with reasonable certainty the kind of progress that you will likely make and you may have to balance this against something more unknown. Of course, the reverse may be the case—you have no idea what even the next year with your current employer will bring and have to put that alongside firm offers and chances from elsewhere

- **Speed of progression:** This needs assessing separately from predictability. For example, my own move out of the publishing industry was based mostly on this factor. However well I might have done I was going to spend too long at the lower levels, not least of earnings, to suit my plan; offered something else attractive, which jumped me forward, I took it. The downside of this could be that what you select produces immediate progress but then a halt; though I have no regrets

- **Future opportunity:** One option may hold out better long-term prospects than another and such decisions should always look well ahead, so far as you are able to do so

- **Current prospects:** These need objective consideration. It is easy to underrate the situation with a current employer when faced with a new opportunity

And of course there is the job itself—both the current one and any other—and all that they entail or might entail. Go back to your objectives. Objectives are dynamic. You do not have to step out of education, form some plans, and then never change them, particularly in a successful career where you may decide to become more and more ambitious. For example, being on the Board may not be among your aspirations early on. Then you do sufficiently well to see being so as actually a real option and a move to achieve that may be exactly what you should then be planning.

It is valid too to see a move as temporary. A common example of this is those people who work for a while overseas, or with an international company, or both, to give themselves this particular kind of experience. Also valid is to consider possible regrets if a course of action is not followed. Again in my own case, when I was setting up my own firm it was, for all sorts of reasons, what I wanted to do. At the same time there were other options. Among everything else, the feeling that if I did not try it I would regret it forevermore ran high, made stronger by the fact that it would probably have been more difficult to do later than it was at the time (this option is rarely easy, but, in my case, so far so good!). As was said earlier, it is no good having a reasonable job but spending your life looking back and saying to yourself, *If only I had . . .* Always remember that you cannot wind the clock back.

Finally, another measure may be useful. It is said that if you are not going forward it is time for a change. Everyone wants a job in which they continue to learn and develop. If a job has ceased to provide this and is now merely repetitive, then it may be time to move on. If you have other offers, consider them carefully and always remember in that case there are three options:

1. Staying, and progressing where you are.

2. Taking an offer that has arisen to go elsewhere.

3. Going out to find someone who will make you an offer.

The last could be harder work than taking something offered and available on a plate, but it could be the best bet in the long run.

BE WELL EQUIPPED TO MOVE

If you stay too long with one organization, you may be regarded as having limited experience (though what recruiters regard as "too long" varies a good deal). Conversely, if you have a C.V. that shows a career record of ceaseless change you may come to be regarded as a "job-hopper" and less attractive because of that. Certainly, it is quite possible that, whatever your circumstances, the time you spend with one employer lets your job-hunting skills atrophy. Career development of the sort discussed here includes positive action to prevent this happening. Several things can be done, among them:

- **Keep your C.V. up to date:** Most job-hunting necessitates having an up-to-date statement of your background, qualifications, and experience; even someone approaching you may want this, and so will recruitment agencies and consultants. These quickly get out of date. It is not sufficient for them to say whom you worked with and your job title; certainly for more recent jobs they should spend some of their limited space describing achievements and what you can do for someone else and how. So make notes, review the document regularly, and update as necessary. Remember: you need a well-constructed and well-written C.V.— it is a selling document and there can be no half-measures. It is either good enough to play its part in getting you a new job or it is useless, just so much waste paper. Incidentally the covering letter that goes with a C.V. is also vital. In both cases, despite all the detailed published advice about them, the prevailing standards are not so high that you cannot score points and differentiate yourself by producing a really good one. Remember too that, while you may keep a standard document on file, you may need to tailor it to each particular job application

- **Keep your interview skills up to date:** This may be more difficult than editing your C.V. but anything you do infrequently tends to be more difficult than something you are able to practice. As a result, some would say it is worth while to apply for a job now and then not because you intend to take it (or at least not on the evidence to hand) but just to give yourself interview practice. I am conscious of the horror this will engender in any recruiter reading this—it is difficult enough to undertake a selection campaign without the picture being clouded by a host of people practicing interview techniques, so I will add that this is very much not something to be overdone; but it is a thought

- **Review the press and keep in touch with agencies:** You need to know what is the state of the market, who is hiring, what rates are being paid, and this too needs an active approach

TAKE ACTION TO MOVE THOROUGHLY AND WELL

Competition for jobs in most economies is often considerable. The points above about keeping up to date are part of the answer, but once you are into the process everything must be done really well. This includes:

- Reading job advertisements or other job descriptions carefully (you do not want to apply for the wrong things or to miss a significant opportunity)

- Writing individually composed covering letters to suit the job (and usually tailoring the C.V. also)

- Filling in *all* of an application form and doing so clearly and thoroughly. (I know much of the information is on the C.V., but recruiters often find it easier to compare options presented in similar form, and so would you.) Do so honestly; the incidence of lies on such forms is high, yet who would hire someone if one such is discovered?

- Preparing for interviews

- Being punctual

- Taking the proceedings seriously

- Handling any follow-up efficiently (they may want additional information)

All this is really only common sense. Try to put yourself in the position of the person attempting to fill a job. It can be a thankless and difficult task, yet there is much hanging on it, and the costs of getting it wrong are certainly high. They expect you to be well turned out; they recognize that few recruitments result in the appointment of anyone who turns out to be much better than was thought, though quite a few transpire the other way around. Make it easy for them to see they are dealing with a professional; that is, someone at some pains to help them make the right decision, and your success rate is likely to be higher. This is very obviously a key area, one of many details, and one where again further reading is likely to be worth while.

ALWAYS LEAVE ON GOOD TERMS

Perhaps a seemingly small and simple point, this can prove invaluable later on, and sometimes much later. No one's time in any organization is entirely positive. You are unlikely to see eye to eye with the boss or others over everything. There will be those who always got right up your nose and others where minor niggles characterized your dealings with them. Then you leave and move on. This is not the time to indulge yourself with righteous indignation, still less revenge—even a single barbed remark in a resignation letter, final reports, or memo may be remembered and quoted later out of context. Leave with good grace. Say something about the good things, of which there were presumably some if you have opted to stay there a while, and do not make anything even remotely like an enemy as you take your leave.

If you ask why, and the temptation for at least some throwaway jibe may be great, the reason is that you never know where your ex-colleagues (and ex-boss, for that matter) will end up. They may move on too. You may need a reference, advice, or information. This is a two-way street, and it may be worth indicating to people you may find useful in future that you hope to keep in touch, and that should they think you can help them in future they should not hesitate to say so. There may be contacts that need active maintenance, people with whom you begin to network, and these need adding to any reminder system you use.

Of course, none of these should be taken as implying that there are bound to be difficulties; there may be few or no problems as you move on. Not that there will not be people with whom you will not easily and naturally keep up contact on either a social or a business basis, or both. That is as it should be, but during the run up to a change, and certainly during the time the change is actually taking place, it is worth a little thought to smooth the path. Do not be like an old friend of mine who landed an excellent new job and moved on. I asked him later if he had left on good terms. "Certainly," he said, "it was all fine right up to the drinks in the office on the day I left. I drank a little too much and poured a beer over the M.D.'s head!" You never know who will be useful in future, so never jeopardise a good relationship inadvertently or for no good reason. Good contacts, and friendships, are too valuable to waste.

DO NOT UNDERESTIMATE THE DIFFICULTY

Countries, economies, and times vary, but if you have to get another job—because your contract has expired, you have been made redundant, or, worst case, you have been fired—do not ever underestimate the time and effort that may be involved in obtaining a new job; certainly the right new job. If the economy is strong, employment high, and skilled and experienced people are in high demand, then there may well be little problem. If not, if luck is against you, then you need to take the appropriate action and do so wisely and fast. A prolonged period of unemployment does not look good on your record and after a while, rightly or wrongly, it gets more difficult for you to interest new employers. They may, understandably, view the gap as suspicious and view other candidates more favorably.

So, what does not underestimating what needs to be done mean? An earlier section made the point about all action taken needing to be done thoroughly and well. Here the point concerns quantity. It is wisely said that searching for a job can be a full time job in itself. There is a difference between being employed and beginning to look for something new with there being no pressure to move on quickly, and having to get another job before the lack of salary begins to seriously affect your life style. Make a real routine of it. Set specific time aside each day (even 9 to 5) and work through all the things to be done. These will include:

- Checking all the media that carry job advertisements (newspapers; management journals; trade, professional: and sectional magazines; websites)

- Contacting any appropriate recruitment agencies or consultants

- Researching the company (some ads may look attractive, but you may not even be clear what business the organization is in; this and other details may be worth checking)

- Writing and tailoring applications; and no doubt completing application forms

- Preparing for interviews you may obtain

- Writing on spec to specific organizations even if they are not currently advertising

- Maintaining contact systematically with your network of people who might be able to help or might know someone else who might help

- Expanding your network of contacts—now is the time to attend all those association meetings and committees that were previously difficult to fit into your diary

- Keeping up to date in any way necessary with the technicalities of your business

- Doing any simple development you can fit in (even reading a business book may be useful)

You cannot really have too many applications out there prospecting for you, and it may be worth setting yourself some targets to make sure that you cast your net wide enough. Certainly you should never stop or slow other activities because you have your sights optimistically on one particular job, even if you are sure things are going well. Organizations can take time—weeks, sometimes months—to make a decision. If you do wait and slow down other activities, and then the answer is negative, the result is simply that you have lost time.

A systematic search will stand the best chance of getting you back into employment promptly and, after all, there is no harm in receiving more than one offer; you can always choose the best.

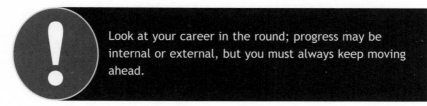

Look at your career in the round; progress may be internal or external, but you must always keep moving ahead.

EXPECT THE UNEXPECTED

What we have been reviewing throughout the book is a process that can be applied over many years, so the things that will happen, the twists and turns of fate that will occur during your career, will be many and varied. You can never anticipate them all. But you may well be able to take advantage of them, provided you have your wits about you.

Many things will occur; I can think of career changes in my own life influenced by factors as varied as the death of a colleague, a chance conversation, a company hitting economic difficulty, the discovery of abilities or possibilities not just that I did not know, but that I had discounted, and unexpected overseas travel. Whatever stage you are at in your career you will no doubt be able to look back on some things that have similarly already had an influence; and there will in all probability be many more to come. Be ready for them. Not specifically, you cannot know what is around the corner, but if you develop the habit of looking for opportunity in everything then some of these random factors can be made to work for you. This, together with a real career plan, can take you forward and, however it may all go in future, can avoid you ever having to look back and regret opportunities ignored or gone by default.

Next, the "Afterword" acts as a summary and checklist to the key principles involved in auditing your career.

afterword

66 If you think you can, you can
and if you think you can't,
you're right. **99**

MARY KAY ASH

Career management should, in a sense, be a full-time job. On the other hand, it is not all-consuming, you do not need to lock yourself in a quiet room to plan and plot for hours on end. The activity that it demands is sometimes formal but, more often, it is simply a matter of an added dimension of consideration during the normal business of getting on with the job in hand. As with so much else in business life, you need to plan and this is a dynamic process. As Sheila Cane and Peter Lowman say in their excellent book *Putting Redundancy Behind You* (published by Kogan Page and representing a good antidote if the worst should happen): *Your personal goals should be reviewed and updated regularly. As your situation changes, it is likely that your personal goals will need to change too.*

Never underestimate change in this context. Successful career management is dependent on forming views and taking actions that are based firmly on the current real situation. Give it no thought for a while, even for the best of reasons—you are busy, content, and everything is going well—and when you next do think about it, picking up the threads may delay or negate action that could make a positive difference to progress.

So think positive. Never rely on good luck; take advantage of it by all means, otherwise it is only useful, as the saying has it, to explain the success of your rivals! And take positive steps that are judged to help the process actively.

TEN KEY ISSUES

After 10 Steps, here we recap and aim to encapsulate the essentials, consolidating what is most useful neatly into (another) ten areas.

1. CONSIDER WHAT SUITS YOU BEST

Your career management is a process to help *you*. Success has no universal definition. It is not based on financial success alone, and it relates to many aspects of work and also, importantly, to personal life. The detail of the analysis that forms the basis for career management decisions and action is dealt with in Step 2; here we concentrate on two key aspects: balance and compromise.

Creating a balance: Career management must be essentially practical. It has to recognize the actual situation about both you and the world in which you work. No one is likely to set their hat successfully at becoming a high flyer in computers if their only experience of a mouse is one that eats cheese. Or at least, if they do, then they must recognize the fundamental hurdles they must overcome and plan and act accordingly.

In looking at such factors as the knowledge and skills you have (or could acquire), your work values, personal characteristics, life outside of work, overall interests and feelings, foibles, and general outlook you must balance what are often very different factors and often be prepared to compromise. Compromise can seem a negative thing, settling for less than you might. Here it is simply a fact of life. Things are not black and white and clashes can occur. To take a simple example: maybe you want to travel. Great. Many careers can, or can be made to, provide this opportunity. But it is not all roses. Living out of a suitcase, time away from home, friends, and family, constant travel, and hotels (even first class ones) can pall. Balance is necessary. Everything needs to be looked at in this way.

If compromise is necessary, then it needs to be a positive one; a mix that, whatever its make-up, suits *you* and about which you are clear. Lack of clarity, running hot and cold, for example one minute acting to maximize travel opportunities and the next to avoid travel getting out of hand, will always hinder your ability to focus and act decisively to create success.

With a balanced view of what you want to achieve in mind, you can line up positive action to achieve just that.

2. SET CLEAR AND SPECIFIC GOALS

To know what you want is basic advice. It is easy, however, to find that a confusion of different possibilities ends up making you fail to concentrate on any one of them, and in such circumstances the route designed to progress your career becomes muddled. So act specifically to ensure clarity of purpose:

- Decide what exactly you want to achieve (there is, in fact, a good deal of detail involved here, as Step 2 sets out)

- Keep your intentions clear in your own mind

- Prioritize your objectives; you may need to decide quickly at some point whether, say, opportunity to travel is more or less important than your earnings

- Review your plans regularly and update them regularly

By all means *aim high*, it is important to do so. But also be prepared to adjust, compromise, and change in light of the situation. If you are clear about yourself, and accommodate the dynamic nature of the world of work—your job, organization, industry, whatever—you will always be well placed to maximize the possibilities of progress in your favor.

3. ACQUIRE AND MAINTAIN THE NECESSARY SKILLS

You may well be good at your job and at the things that make it possible for you to do it well. More likely, you have some gaps— things you are not quite so good at doing. Almost certainly you will also have gaps to come, indeed gaps you can predict. The last is no reflection on you; it is just that things move on. New skills come on the scene—nowhere more than in matters of computers and information technology—and others simply become more important to you. For example, one day your job may involve nothing in terms of negotiation, then changes in the job—positive ones—can mean that this is an inherent part of what you must do in future. And you simply have to understand it and do it well.

The job here is simply stated. You must:

- Recognize the importance of competencies and their role in your success

- Assess what you must be able to do now and whether your level of competency should be improved (either to hit a satisfactory level, or to excel and create advantage)

- Take action to obtain any kind of development help that might be needed

- Anticipate and predict how things might change and what new skills this might need you to add or augment

- Take action to deal with this well in advance (letting events overtake you can create considerable disadvantage)

- Make a virtue of the process (bosses tend to respect those who want to keep themselves up to date—but stress the advantages to the *organization* as much as, or more than, to you)

4. DO A GOOD JOB

Two points need to be made here. First, and more obvious, is the fact that doing a good job in whatever role you have currently is normally a necessary foundation to progress. There are incompetents that get on (perhaps you work for one!), but it is not the rule. The previous point about development is important here; you have to work at creating a suitable competency as well as at managing your career.

Secondly, you have to be sure that your success is noticed. You cannot hide your light under a bushel and hope to have people rushing to promote you. Your success needs recording and publicizing; both are worth comment:

- Keep a personal record of your successes, and keep it in writing (together with any documentation). This is invaluable for a number of reasons, internal and external. Two key ones are preparing for appraisals and keeping your C.V. up to date

- Seek opportunities to publicize your successes, something that can involve every communications channel that exists, from grapevine to formal meetings

But there is an important caveat here: you must undertake this activity on a carefully considered basis. The line between gradually giving people—the right people—a building picture that makes them aware of how you are doing, and what you can do, and being seen as a pompous, self-centered pain in the butt is a narrow one. So think carefully, do not exaggerate in a way that will instantly be seen through or otherwise overdo things. Try too to do things that have another reason for them beyond just saying "I'm great"; for example, you might want to point out how some recent experience fits you to assist with a project. If so, doing so in terms of *helping the project* may well make most sense. Providing information, yet maintaining acceptability makes for a good maxim here.

5. CULTIVATE THE APPROPRIATE PROFILE

The profile you have within your own organization, indeed around the total range of circles within which you move, is a *significant* part of what may act as a catalyst to success. You may be knowledgable, decisive, competent, and more—but what do people think? For example, how do you come over at meetings? It is not just the ideas or opinions you express that are important, it is also just *how* you express them. If you are seen as having no ideas, no influence—or no patience, this may be significant.

There is a wide range of things to think about here; however, detail apart, the key issues are:

- To be clear how you want to be perceived

- To stress or minimize characteristics in a way that helps create and maintain the profile that you want

- To be ever-sensitive to the fine line between posing and simply acting to make good things clear

Action is necessary for most of us in this kind of area; and a balanced approach is best.

6. USE THE SYSTEMS THAT CAN HELP EFFECTIVELY

Career management is not all about what you do alone and unaided. Of course many of the things that help are individual actions and many occur through the normal day-to-day activity of your work, utilizing what goes on in a project meeting for instance.

But there are a number of systems and processes that go on in an organization that can help you; indeed, there are some that have helping you as part of their reason for existence. Use them, and aim to get the most from them. The most obvious are:

- **Job appraisal:** Almost all organizations have a formal system to evaluate people and help prompt good performance in future. They should be constructive, certainly the best attitude to have to them is that they are—act accordingly and get the most from them

- **Training and development:** Most organizations have some training resources (and many also make use of external ones). Check them out. Make sure that you are benefiting from all they have to offer; the importance of skills was the subject of point three above. You do not have to go on a course to extend your development; there are many other options such as e-learning, or just reading up on something, which you can fit in. There are low-cost options that you can get sanction for if their cost needs to be put into a suitable budget

7. DOCUMENT WHERE NECESSARY

Think of something that you were doing two years back and consider how it will help you in future. Who was the guy from head office you spoke to last month and who said always to let him know if you were in town? The details may already be sketchy after a month, never mind two years. So this is a straightforward overall maxim to resolve to keep.

- Keep good records

- Keep them up to date

- Use a system that lets you find things reliably and easily

- Review your records regularly (and clean and update them; but carefully)

Details range from names, contact details, and what someone is, does, or how they might be useful to "exhibits." The last might range from a report filed following an appraisal to something you have done that shows your prowess (a particularly well-crafted report or a write up about you in the company newsletter). If you take a little time and trouble to do this progressively, it saves time—and missed opportunities—in the longer term.

8. DEAL WITH PEOPLE—FRIEND AND FOE

There are two kinds of people that are relevant to career management (not counting those who inhabit positions or have characteristics that affect things not at all). There are those that can help and those that hinder. And it is worth noting that they may do either wittingly or unwittingly.

One important person is your immediate boss. As to others, the possibilities are endless. People you need to relate to in some way or another include those in and outside the organization, people at different levels of the hierarchy—specifically above and below you, people you work with, and those with whom you simply cross paths. It includes those with obvious influence and those who can help in more subtle ways. And there may be a fair number of them. So:

- Keep in touch and keep details of people (it is just when you are unable to find the details of the guy you sat next to at a residential conference two years back that something happens to make them the best person to help)

- Network effectively. You need reasons to be in touch, reasons that are as valid for others as for you. Successful networking creates a relationship and that needs work to maintain

- Be generous. Networking is a two-way street, you get out in proportion to what you put in. Say thank you and be prepared to take time to help others

- Be open-minded about people. Anyone may be useful, anyone may represent some future danger—check it out

Whom you know really is as important as what you know.

9. MANAGE THE POLITICS OF ORGANIZATIONS

Always remember that organizations are the sum total of the people in them, and that people operate for all sorts of motivations both positively and negatively. The office without office politics has not been invented, much of what goes on is competitive, and some of it is, for want of a better word, spoiling.

Competition may be straightforwardly that. Fair enough. If more than one person is after a particular promotion, then may the best one win and, all things being equal, that is what will happen. But, unsurprisingly, all things never are equal. So the range of what may happen is considerable. There are people who regard the maxim *all's fair in love and war* as precisely right for the office. They are not adverse to an unfair advantage and will act not just unfairly, but sometimes dishonestly, to get an advantage any way they can. Others, perhaps seeing that they will miss out, enjoy sabotaging others and spoiling their chances.

In a sense the reasons for all this do not matter. What does matter is recognizing that it happens. You may not want to open a turf war, but you may well want to take preemptive action.

Alternatively—and just as important—it is possible that political alliances may have positive effect. Even something as simple as someone putting in a good word for you, or thinking to alert you to an opportunity, may be enough to make the difference between success and failure. So what attitude should you take to all this?

- Never forget that office politics exist

- Avoid getting involved in the negative aspects of office politics, which can do damage to your profile

- Monitor the situation and the people carefully to anticipate either opportunities or situations or people to guard against

- Use the unofficial communications channels and alliances with people, including those distanced from you by functional or hierarchical boundaries, to your advantage

Overall, don't panic, but try to keep ahead of the game—these things may cause little difficulty, but the stage on which your career plans are played out will probably have some adversarial aspects.

10. WATCH FOR AND TAKE ADVANTAGE OF OPPORTUNITIES

For all that career management is an active process, serendipity is likely to be part of what makes things happen for you. You are in the right place at the right time, you happen to see or hear something first, events take an unexpected turn—there are so many ways in which things can happen that have no relationship whatever to your careful planning. Can you influence this sort of thing? Yes. Certainly if you are actively managing your career you may well create your own luck; indeed, it may well be difficult to trace back the cause, or, more likely, causes. Why does an approach from another organization, or a headhunter, come out of the blue? Perhaps it is the result of a whole series of things, someone you sat next to at a conference, an article you had published in a trade journal, what an external contact, a supplier perhaps, says about you—you may well never know.

So the first principle here is that systematic career management does not just make it more likely that the specific things you aim at will happen, it can prompt unimagined things too. It is possible that it is one of these that produces a real break.

But there may be more that you can do, for example:

- Watch out for opportunities: first, by keeping a clear head and not getting so bogged down in what you are doing that you see nothing else; secondly, by making connections about the things you do see

- Put yourself in a position to have something to observe: this may involve all sorts of things from attending meetings or conferences to just taking the time and trouble to keep in touch with contacts who might be useful in the future

When something unforeseen does occur, do not grab at it in unconsidered delight. You may rue the day. Rather take a considered view just as you should of any other possible course of action and consider both the positive and negative aspects of it. Then decide and if it is to go for something—do just that, wholeheartedly.

Remember one further thing as you do so: work at making your working life *enjoyable*.

FINALLY . . .

There is a danger that thinking about the nature of career management and what needs to be done to take an active approach to it, may blind one to one key, underlying factor. Of course, work is the main source of income for most people, and on that depends your personal security and ability to lead the kind of life you want. But work is a part of life. For many people it is something on which you spend a very considerable number of hours; more if you add the time it takes to get to and from work.

So surely getting satisfaction—enjoyment—from work is a key objective. At the end of the day the active approach that you take must balance progress, in the sense of position, responsibility, salary, and so on, against what you get from work in other ways. Sometimes there are compromises to be made in this respect, and if there are then so be it. You must decide:

- What you rate most highly

- How you are going to see this balance

- How you want it to manifest itself

Then you must direct your action accordingly; and here it is worth restating the ten questions listed at the start of this book:

1. Do you know what you want?

2. Are you aiming high?

3. Is your work environment progress-friendly?

4. Are people you work with and for a career asset?

5. Do you have the skills to progress?

6. Is your profile appropriate for what you want to do?

7. Do you enjoy what you do as much as you wish?

8. Do you get adequately rewarded?

9. Are you ready for action?

10. Do you have an action plan?

Your answering all of these constitutes a useful audit of your career. The answers will condition the plan you make and the action you take. You will never know exactly where your plan will take you, that is the nature of life. However, perhaps one thing is more important than any other. That is avoiding, at some point in the future, having to say to yourself something that begins with the words *If only . . .*

So, never assume all will be plain sailing. Never stop looking for opportunities. See your career plan, and the management of it, as a living entity, not something cast in stone—and aim high.

Whatever you have done in the past, keep it in your memory and learn from it. The future, however, is in your imagination; work at it, go for it, and make it happen. It would be inappropriate after all that has been said here to end by wishing you good luck, but I wish you well with it.

ABOUT THE AUTHOR

Patrick Forsyth has himself had a successful career; or certainly he likes to think so. He now runs his own company, Touchstone Training & Consultancy, specializing in the improvement of marketing, sales, and communications skills, and says he has now *found an employer I can really get on with*.

He began his career in publishing and worked happily in sales, in promotion and marketing there before escaping to something better paid just ahead of terminal poverty. He then worked for the Institute of Marketing (now the Chartered Institute) first in research, latterly in the promotion of their training products and publications. He helped set up an export assistance scheme and then moved into consultancy, first in a management marketing position. Much against his better judgment initially, he was soon persuaded to get involved in client work and began to undertake consulting assignments and conduct training courses.

His work also began to take on an international dimension. He helped set up offices in Brussels and Singapore and began to work and lecture overseas. He still travels regularly, especially to South East Asia, and has, over the years, worked in most countries in continental Europe, including the former Eastern bloc. Other, more occasional, visits have included America, Australia, East Africa, Argentina, and Borneo.

After some years at director level in a medium-sized marketing consultancy, he set up his own organization in 1990. He conducts training for organizations in a wide range of industries, and has conducted public courses for such bodies as the Institute of Management, the City University Business School, and the London Chamber of Commerce and Industry.

In addition, he writes on matters of management and marketing in a variety of business journals and is the author of more than 50 business books (with titles published in more than 20 languages). These include: *Manage Your Boss* (also from Cyan in this series),

Powerful Reports and Proposals, and *Successful Time Management* (both from Kogan Page). He has also written corporate publications and material to accompany a variety of training packages (audio, video, etc.) and has appeared on television discussing marketing and management (fame at last?—with one broadcast in association with the Executive Business Channel/BBC Open University at 3 a.m.!).

His early career plans included "avoiding public speaking and writing" (so nothing goes perfectly). Future plans include "less work and more money" (so the trend is likely to continue). Nothing like this book was around early in his career; or who knows what he might have done. Whatever else, he says he is able to look back at a career that has been "almost wholly very enjoyable"; and which continues to be so.

OTHER TITLES IN THE CAREER MAKERS SERIES

ISBN 981 261 820 1 (Asia & ANZ)

ISBN 1-904879-53-5

UK £12.99 • USA $23.95 • CAN $32.95

OTHER TITLES IN THE CAREER MAKERS SERIES

ISBN 981 261 821 X (Asia & ANZ)

ISBN 1-904879-52-7

UK £12.99 • USA $23.95 • CAN $32.95